Walt DISNEY WORLD

by Hannah Gramson

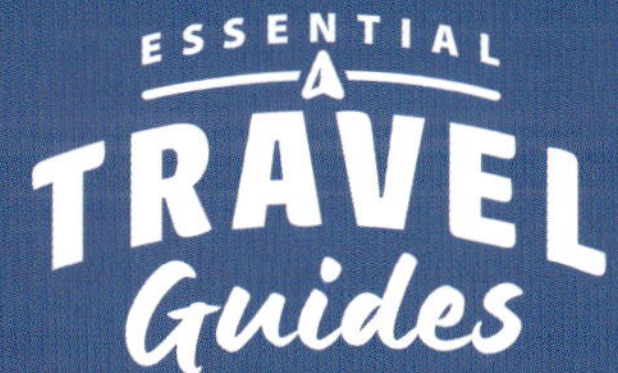

Essential Library

An Imprint of Abdo Publishing
abdobooks.com

ABDOBOOKS.COM

Published by Abdo Publishing, a division of ABDO, PO Box 398166, Minneapolis, Minnesota 55439.

Printed in China.
052025
092025

Cover Photo: Dennis MacDonald/Alamy
Interior Photos: Florida Development Commission/Department of Commerce Collection/Florida Memory, 4–5; Hulton Archive/Archive Photos/Getty Images, 8; Earl Theisen Collection/Archive Photos/Getty Images, 11; AP Images, 12, 15; Roberto Machado Noa/LightRocket/Getty Images, 16–17, 24; AaronP/Bauer-Griffin/GC Images/Getty Images, 18, 60–61; Joni Hanebutt/Alamy, 22, 27; M2 Photography/Alamy, 25; Greg Balfour Evans/Alamy, 30–31; Joseph Prezioso/Anadolu Agency/Getty Images, 32–33; Junior Braz/Shutterstock Images, 34; Viridescent Visuals/Alamy, 37; Gerardo Mora/Getty Images Entertainment/Getty Images, 39, 77; Jeffrey Whyte/Alamy, 42; Matt Stroshane/Disney Parks/Getty Images Entertainment/Getty Images, 44; America/Alamy, 47; Andrew Barker/Alamy, 48–49, 65; VIAVAL/Alamy, 52, 80; Shutterstock Images, 54, 58, 72–73, 83, 84–85; Camila Romeiro/Shutterstock Images, 57; Gustavo Caballero/Getty Images Entertainment/Getty Images, 66; Charles Sykes/Invision/AP Images, 69; Marc Rasmus/imageBROKER.com GmbH & Co. KG/Alamy, 70; Buff Henry Photography/Alamy, 78; M. Timothy O'Keefe/Alamy, 86; Thomas Marchessault/Alamy, 89; Lucy Clark/Alamy Live News/Alamy, 90; Craig Russell/Alamy, 92–93; Mark Ashman/Disney Parks/Getty Images Entertainment/Getty Images, 96; Joshua Moore/iStockphoto, 99; Red Line Editorial, 101

Editor: Laura Stickney
Series Designer: Joshua Olson

Library of Congress Control Number: 2024948597

PUBLISHER'S CATALOGING-IN-PUBLICATION DATA

Names: Gramson, Hannah, author.
Title: Walt Disney World / by Hannah Gramson
Description: Minneapolis, Minnesota: Abdo Publishing, 2026 | Series: Essential travel guides | Includes online resources and index.
Identifiers: ISBN 9781098297114 (lib. bdg.) | ISBN 9798384919636 (ebook)
Subjects: LCSH: Walt Disney World (Fla.)--Juvenile literature. | Travel--Juvenile literature. | United States--Guidebooks--Juvenile literature. | Amusement parks--Juvenile literature. | Historic sites--Juvenile literature.
Classification: DDC 917.592--dc23

CONTENTS

CHAPTER ONE
THE HISTORY OF WALT DISNEY WORLD 4

CHAPTER TWO
MAGIC KINGDOM 16

CHAPTER THREE
EPCOT 32

CHAPTER FOUR
HOLLYWOOD STUDIOS 48

CHAPTER FIVE
ANIMAL KINGDOM 60

CHAPTER SIX
HIDDEN GEMS 72

CHAPTER SEVEN
HOTELS AND DINING 84

CHAPTER EIGHT
HOLIDAYS AND FESTIVALS 92

ESSENTIAL FACTS 100
GLOSSARY 102
ADDITIONAL RESOURCES 104
SOURCE NOTES 106
INDEX 110
ABOUT THE AUTHOR 112

CHAPTER
ONE

THE HISTORY OF WALT DISNEY WORLD

In 1964, a group of mysterious men arrived in central Florida and started asking local landowners about purchasing their land. The area consisted mainly of farmland and undeveloped swampland. It was located about 20 miles (32 km) south of a small city called Orlando.[1] Among the men looking to purchase land were brothers Walt and Roy Davis. The land they were seeking to buy was for something they called Project X.

Rumors soon started to fly. Many people thought the men must work for a major company or organization that was planning to move to the area. But what was it? Did they work for Ford Motors? Or perhaps the men worked for Boeing, the world's largest aerospace company?

In 1965, Walt and Roy Disney attended a press conference in Orlando, Florida, with the state's governor, W. Haydon Burns. During the conference, the brothers officially announced their plans to build Walt Disney World.

On October 24, 1965, a reporter for the *Orlando Sentinel* cracked the case. The headline on the front page of that day's newspaper read "We Say: 'Mystery' Industry Is Disney."[2] Walt and Roy Davis were, in fact, Walt and Roy Disney. They had spent nearly a year buying up land in central Florida, where they planned to build what would become the world's largest theme park: Walt Disney World.

To keep their plans secret, the Disney brothers never personally contacted landowners in central Florida. Instead, using made-up company names, they had other people quietly buy up the land. Their business partners used false names to conceal their identities. When Walt or Roy traveled to the area themselves, they used the fake last name "Davis." This way, their initials would still match their monogrammed suitcases.

Going Undercover

Using false names wasn't the only tactic the Disney brothers and their business partners used to conceal their identities and keep their plans secret. When headed to central Florida, they would arrange flights into other cities before going to their destination. One man went so far as to be coached in the regional accent so people would think he was a local. But his cover was blown when he mispronounced the name of a small town called Kissimmee. He pronounced it "*Kiss*-a-me" instead of "Ka-*sim*-ee."

Even within the Disney company, the project was

kept a secret. Aside from the Disney brothers, only five other people knew about Project X. If anyone outside the company had known what they were up to, the value of the land they were hoping to buy would have skyrocketed. The company bought the main tract of land for about $145 an acre.[3] This is equal to about $1,475 in 2024.[4] After Disney was revealed as the buyer, land prices rose to $1,000 an acre.[5] This would be about $10,016 in 2024.[6]

> **"There's enough land here to hold all the ideas and plans we can possibly imagine.[8]"**
> ***—Walt Disney, on the building plans for Walt Disney World***

By the end of 1965, Disney had purchased about 43 square miles (111 sq km) of land in central Florida. That's nearly the size of the city of San Francisco, California. It's almost twice the size of Manhattan in New York City.[7]

A Boy with a Dream

Long before Walt and Roy started buying land in central Florida, Disney had become a household name. Walt Disney was born on December 5, 1901, in Chicago, Illinois. But he spent most of his childhood on a farm near Marceline, Missouri. Growing up, Walt was a creative boy with an incredible imagination. He often drew cartoons

Walt Disney came up with the idea for Mickey Mouse during a train ride from New York to California. He originally named the character Mortimer, but his wife convinced him to change the name to Mickey.

in his school notebooks. Once, he even got in trouble for using black tar to paint pictures on the side of his family's white house. Walt dreamed of working in film and the growing animation industry.

Although Roy was eight years older than Walt, the brothers were very close. In 1923, they moved to Hollywood, California, where they started the Disney Brothers Cartoon Studio. Just five years later, Walt introduced the world to Disney's most iconic character:

Mickey Mouse. *Steamboat Willie*, the first Mickey Mouse cartoon to be shown to the public, premiered at the Colony Theater in New York City on November 18, 1928. It was an immediate hit.

Over the next few decades, Disney created some of the most iconic films in US history. One was *Snow White and the Seven Dwarfs*, which was released in 1937. It was the first feature-length animated film to be made in the United States. Many people expected the film to fail. They didn't think anyone would pay to watch an 80-minute cartoon. Even Walt's wife, Lillian, who worked as an animator for Disney, thought the film would fail. Roy thought so too.

But *Snow White* became a massive success. It marked a turning point for the Disney company, earning Walt a reputation as one of the most innovative filmmakers of all time. Walt went on to win 26 Academy Awards for

A Special Award

Despite the success of *Snow White and the Seven Dwarfs*, the movie couldn't be nominated in the Academy Awards' Best Picture category. This is because it was an animated film. However, in 1938, Walt won a special Academy Award for the movie. It featured one standard-size Oscar statue accompanied by seven miniature statues. These represented the dwarfs in the film. It is one of only two customized Oscar awards ever made.[9]

his films.[10] In 2024, he still held the record for the most Oscars won by a single person.

In the early 1940s, Walt started making plans to build an amusement park and offer tours through a movie set near his film studio in Burbank, California. By 1952, he had formed WED Enterprises to begin building the park on studio grounds. But eventually, Walt decided to build the park in the small town of Anaheim, California, where there was more space available. With more land, Walt started to think of the amusement park as a giant movie set that would be open to the public. In 1954, construction began on the park now known as Disneyland.

Building Walt Disney World

When the news broke that the Disney company was buying up land in central Florida, locals were thrilled. Right away, many guessed that he was planning to build an East Coast version of the world-renowned Disneyland theme park. But Walt wasn't planning to build just another Disneyland. He wanted to build a bigger, better theme park unlike anything the world had ever seen before.

Disneyland, which had opened in 1955, had been a major success. US amusement parks such as Lake Compounce in Connecticut and Cedar Point in Ohio had offered visitors thrilling rides, fun games, and exciting exhibits since the mid-1800s. But Disneyland was something entirely new. The park was themed around fantasy stories and fairy tales, and it featured the characters and worlds depicted in Disney's movies. Within the first ten weeks of opening, Disneyland received one million visitors. By 1960, five million people were visiting the park each year.[11]

While planning Disneyland, Walt Disney, *left*, and his team made illustrations and models of rides and buildings. One model was of the park's Sleeping Beauty Castle.

Because of Disneyland, Anaheim had grown from a small town of about 20,000 people into a city of 160,000 people in just a couple of years. Leaders across the country urged Walt to build a similar theme park in their cities. But he resisted, reportedly saying, "I don't get much kick out of doing something twice."[12]

However, the success of Disneyland came with a downside. Hotels, restaurants, and stores not owned by

Walt Disney World's Magic Kingdom was photographed while under construction in July 1971. The park was not fully complete on its opening day in October of that year.

Disney had sprung up, crowding around the park and leaving no room for Disneyland to expand. This upset Walt, who felt that it "broke the illusion" of his park.[13] The idea of a new park—one that was bigger and better than the original—became more appealing.

In 1958, Walt and a few others at his company started planning for a new park. Although Disneyland received millions of visitors each year, only about 2 percent came from east of the Mississippi River.[14] Walt wanted the new park to be more accessible for families on the East Coast, so the company began scouting areas in that region. Finally, in 1963, Walt decided central Florida would be the perfect home for his new park.

Walt chose central Florida for several reasons. First, vast areas of inexpensive land were available there—enough land for the park to continue to expand for years

From Mud to Magic

Because much of the land purchased for Disney World was swampland, the park's designers ran into some major problems. First, they had to build more than 43 miles (69 km) of canals to regulate water levels in the soil.[15] Then, when it was time to break ground on the site, they discovered that a large swath of the land was too marshy for construction. Luckily, one of the designers came up with a clever solution. They would transform that part of the land into a 200-acre (81 ha) lagoon.[16] Today, some of the most popular hotels at Walt Disney World line the shores of this lagoon.

to come. Second, two major roadways intersected nearby, which would make driving to the park easy for visitors. Finally, the weather in central Florida was perfect. It was sunny and warm for most of the year, even in winter.

The Opening of Walt Disney World

Sadly, Walt didn't live to see his new park open. He passed away from lung cancer on December 15, 1966. Many people worried about what Walt's death would mean for the park. Would the company move forward with the project? Was it even possible to accomplish it without Walt working behind the scenes?

At the time, Walt's brother Roy had been planning to retire. But the project to build the new park had been important to Walt. Roy decided to postpone his retirement and take over the project's planning, determined to see it through. The company broke ground on the site in 1967, and construction began a few years later, in 1969. The park took about 18 months to build, costing roughly $400 million.[17] That's equal to around $3.1 billion in 2024.[18]

The park opened on October 1, 1971, welcoming more than 10,000 visitors on its first day. It was, and continues to be, the largest theme park in the world. It's also the most visited, with more than 58 million visitors each year.[19]

A grand opening ceremony was held at Walt Disney World from October 23 to October 25, 1971. The ceremony included a parade with a marching band and costumed characters.

Originally, Walt had planned to name the park Disney World. However, in memory of Walt, Roy insisted that the park's official name be *Walt* Disney World. The park welcomed millions of annual visitors with signs that read "Walt Disney World: Where Dreams Come True." In 2021, the signs were changed to read "The Most Magical Place on Earth."[20]

CHAPTER
TWO

MAGIC KINGDOM

When Walt Disney World opened in 1971, it contained only one park: Magic Kingdom. Today, Magic Kingdom is one of four parks at Walt Disney World, but it remains the most popular. In fact, by itself, it has more visitors annually than any other theme park in the world.

In the middle of Magic Kingdom is one of the most iconic structures found in Walt Disney World: Cinderella Castle. Six paths branch off from the castle. Each leads to one of the themed lands that make up Magic Kingdom. These are Main Street, U.S.A.; Liberty Square; Adventureland; Frontierland; Tomorrowland; and Fantasyland. Each land offers a unique experience, with restaurants, exhibits, shops, and rides all centered on a theme.

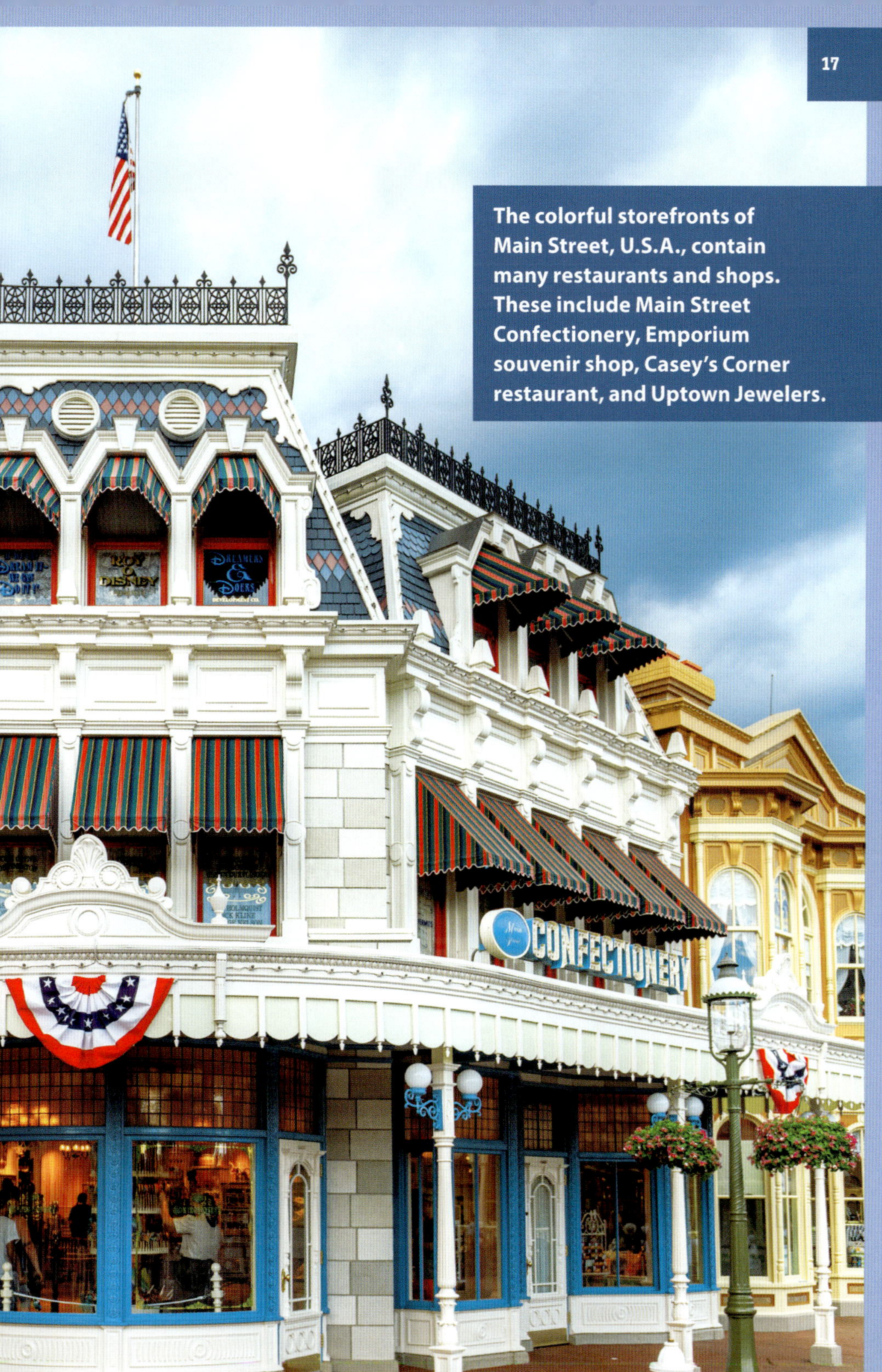

The colorful storefronts of Main Street, U.S.A., contain many restaurants and shops. These include Main Street Confectionery, Emporium souvenir shop, Casey's Corner restaurant, and Uptown Jewelers.

Don't Miss It!

Cinderella Castle

When people think of Walt Disney World, the first image that comes to mind is often of Cinderella Castle. Sitting at the heart of Magic Kingdom, this castle is one of the most iconic buildings in the park. The castle was modeled after Neuschwanstein Castle in Schwangau, Germany. Cinderella Castle has 27 towers, a stone bridge, and a water-filled moat.[1]

At the time the castle was built, federal flight safety laws stated that any building taller than 190 feet (58 m) must have a blinking red light at the top. Because this would spoil the fairy-tale feel of the building, Cinderella Castle is only 189 feet (58 m) tall.[2] But builders used a technique called forced perspective to make the castle look much taller. The bricks and windows toward the top of the castle are smaller than those at the bottom. From the ground, this makes it look like the castle is a lot taller than it really is.

Another magical detail about Cinderella Castle is that it is designed to always look good in photographs. This is because the castle was built facing south, so the sun is never behind it. There are also no nearby buildings that can cast shadows over the castle.

Disney employees, or cast members, appear throughout each land dressed as popular Disney characters.

Main Street, U.S.A.

Every visitor who passes through the front gates of Walt Disney World must walk down Main Street, U.S.A. to reach the rest of the park. This area of Magic Kingdom was designed to look like a small, prosperous East Coast resort town in the early 1900s. Some of the buildings on the street are modeled after those in Walt's hometown of Marceline, Missouri.

Many visitors think strolling down Main Street, U.S.A. feels like traveling back in time. Old-fashioned lampposts and buildings with colorful early-1900s architecture line the street. Horse-drawn trolleys, old-fashioned buses, horseless carriages, and even an antique fire engine carry guests around the area. Along Main Street, visitors can find restaurants, souvenir shops, a bakery, a candy store, and an ice cream shop. There's even a barbershop where visitors can get haircuts.

The buildings of Main Street, U.S.A. are full of references to Walt Disney's films and life. Knowledgeable Disney fans can spot these details. In front of Tony's Town Square Restaurant, for instance, visitors can find two paw prints inside a heart etched into the pavement. This is a reference to the Disney movie *Lady and the Tramp.* A sign over one of the Emporium shop's entrances reads "Established in 1901."[3] This is the year Walt Disney was born. The second-story windows of many buildings along the street have names printed on the glass. These are the names of people who played important roles in the Disney company and in the building of Walt Disney World.

Liberty Square

Park guests can travel even further back in time by visiting Liberty Square, which is modeled after a Colonial-era town. The Colonial era spanned from 1607 to 1775. During this time, the United States was not a country yet. It consisted of 13 colonies ruled by Great Britain. The colonies fought against the British in the American Revolutionary War (1775–1783) to gain independence.

Liberty Square contains many clever references to US history. For example, there are two lanterns hanging in the second-story window of a house along the street. This is a reference to a 1775 event involving Paul Revere, who rode on horseback to warn colonists that British soldiers were coming. Two lanterns were hung in a church steeple to warn people that British soldiers were arriving by sea.

The centerpiece of Liberty Square is the Liberty Square Tree. This is a real tree that park engineers moved from elsewhere in the park. They carried it to its current location using a giant crane. The tree's branches hold 13 lanterns, which symbolize the 13 original colonies. A replica of the Liberty Bell is found in the square too.

One popular attraction in Liberty Square is the Hall of Presidents. This is inside a building that looks like Independence Hall, a building in Philadelphia, Pennsylvania. The Declaration of Independence was signed there. The Hall of Presidents attraction begins with a film that explains how the United States came to be.

The film discusses important events in the country's history. After the film, the screen rises to reveal realistic audio-animatronic figures of every US president. An audio-animatronic is a robot that can move and

Answer the Phone!

There are many hidden gems and details throughout Walt Disney World. One hidden gem in Main Street, U.S.A. is an old-fashioned crank telephone inside a store called the Chapeau. If a visitor picks up the phone, they can listen to a prerecorded conversation between some nosy neighbors exchanging gossip. This is a throwback to the time when phones had party lines. Up to 20 households would share the same phone line, which meant people could eavesdrop on each other's private conversations.[4]

make sound. If visitors look closely, they might see the presidents blinking and nodding.

Liberty Square is also home to the Haunted Mansion, one of the most beloved rides in Walt Disney World. It takes place in a large, detailed mansion. The ride follows the story of Constance Hatchaway, a bride whose many husbands have mysteriously died. Before visitors enter the house, the ride's queue leads them through a graveyard with tombstones, busts, and interactive crypts. Guests can touch parts of the crypts to make music play or trigger special effects.

The Haunted Mansion queue leads visitors past six busts of characters from the fictional Dread family. Visitors can study the busts and read the epitaphs on their pedestals to try to solve the mystery of how each character died.

Many of the names on the gravestones are the names of Imagineers, or Disney engineers, who helped design and build the attraction. Once inside, visitors hitch a ride in a "Doom Buggy." The buggy takes them through the mansion, where they encounter dozens of ghosts. The ride is full of spooky details such as hidden faces, glowing footprints, and door knockers that move on their own.

Frontierland

As visitors pass through Liberty Square into Frontierland, they are transported to the Wild West. This land is built to look like a town on the western frontier in the 1800s, when Americans were first starting to settle west of the Mississippi River. The buildings in Frontierland look rustic, and banjo music plays daily. Visitors can buy souvenirs such as leather goods and wood carvings. Shops in the area are designed to look like old trading posts.

Audio-Animatronics at Disney

Walt Disney found an antique mechanical bird while on vacation in New Orleans, Louisiana. He thought his team at Disney could build something similar. The team took the bird apart and studied its mechanics. They built a prototype of a human animatronic. The team went on to create the world's first audio-animatronic human figure. It was of US president Abraham Lincoln. Today, there are around 6,000 animatronics throughout Disney parks worldwide.[5]

The design of Big Thunder Mountain Railroad was inspired by ghost towns of the Wild West and by red rock formations found in the southwestern United States.

One of the most iconic rides in Frontierland is Big Thunder Mountain Railroad. It is a roller coaster with cars designed to look like train cars. The ride carries passengers through the Big Thunder Mountain Mining Company town before taking them into a fake mine that lies deep within a large, rocky mountain. The ride zips into, out of, and over the mountain, flying past scenes of animals and miners at work.

One of the newest attractions in Frontierland is Tiana's Bayou Adventure, a log flume ride. It opened in 2024, replacing an older ride called Splash Mountain. Tiana's Bayou Adventure is inspired by the 2009 animated

Disney film *The Princess and the Frog*. The ride takes place in a large fake mountain with a waterfall. Some parts of the ride take place inside the mountain, while others take place outside. Riders hop into floating cars shaped like logs. They journey deep into a Louisiana bayou full of audio-animatronic jazz musicians, including a trumpet-playing alligator. The ride ends with a splash after a 50-foot (15 m) drop down the mountain's waterfall.[6]

Adventureland

The next stop in Magic Kingdom is Adventureland. This land is inspired by the jungles, deserts, and tropical islands of several places around the world, including Africa, Asia, the Caribbean, the Middle East, and Polynesia. One of the most popular rides in Adventureland is the Jungle Cruise. It is a riverboat cruise ride. Visitors board a replica of a

The 15 boats on the Jungle Cruise ride have names inspired by rivers around the world. Examples include *Ucyali Lolly, Amazon Annie*, and *Congo Connie*.

1930s boat. Then they voyage through the jungles of Africa and Asia. A cast member dressed as a riverboat skipper narrates the ride, often making silly jokes.

Along the way, riders encounter dozens of lifelike animatronic animals in and along the river. These include zebras, lions, elephants, giraffes, and hippos. Riders also see buildings and animatronic scenes, such as a group of explorers climbing a tree to escape a rhinoceros.

Smellitizers

To make guests' experiences more authentic, Walt Disney World has scent-emitting machines known as "Smellitizers" installed around the park. On Main Street, U.S.A., these machines pump out the scent of fresh popcorn and baked goods. Smellitizers at the Haunted Mansion make it smell like a dusty attic and cedar beams. On the Pirates of the Caribbean ride, the air is filled with the scent of gunpowder and wet wood. In some areas, garlic extract is pumped in to ward off mosquitoes.

Another well-known attraction in Adventureland is Pirates of the Caribbean. This ride inspired the popular movie franchise of the same name. The ride takes place indoors and is based on pirates in the 1700s and 1800s.

After boarding a boat, riders float past a large rock formation shaped like a skull before heading into a cave. Then they find themselves in the middle of a pirate attack on a Caribbean port city. The ride takes visitors past many animatronic scenes of pirate life. In 2006, the ride was updated to include characters from the movie franchise.

The Astro Orbiter ride is in the center of Tomorrowland. Riders sit in elevated rocket-shaped cars and spin around large models of planets.

Tomorrowland

Tomorrowland is another land in Magic Kingdom. It is all about space exploration, technological advancements, and the future. Originally, Tomorrowland was modeled after Walt's idea of what the future might look like. But as the real world changed, so did Tomorrowland. In the 1990s, the land was redesigned to depict the future imagined by science fiction writers of the 1920s and 1930s. Just about everything in Tomorrowland is made of neon, glass, and shiny metal—including the palm trees.

In Tomorrowland, visitors can go on some of Walt Disney World's most popular rides, including Buzz Lightyear's Space Ranger Spin. This shooting gallery ride, which features *Toy Story* characters, is designed to make park visitors feel as if they're the size of toys. They go inside a video game to help Buzz Lightyear battle the evil alien Emperor Zurg, who is stealing batteries from other toys. During the ride, riders can try to hit targets with laser beams.

Tomorrowland is also home to Walt Disney's Carousel of Progress—an attraction older than Walt Disney World itself. The carousel is part ride and part show. The audience sits in seats that rotate around a center stage. The show is made of four short plays that feature audio-animatronic characters. The plays depict how daily life and technology have changed through the 1900s. The original version of the carousel was built for the New York World's Fair of 1964 to 1965, seven years before Walt Disney World opened.

Space Mountain, one of Walt Disney World's most intense and thrilling rides, can also be found in Tomorrowland. Built a few years after the park opened, Space Mountain quickly became a fan favorite. The roller coaster is housed inside a 180-foot (55 m) metal mountain.[7] After boarding a rocket-shaped car, riders shoot through almost complete darkness on a track with unexpected drops and turns. Meanwhile, comets, stars, and other space objects whiz by. The ride's features were inspired by real-life space exploration. A former astronaut helped develop the ride's design. Space Mountain was such a hit at Walt Disney World that the ride was later added to Disneyland.

Fantasyland

Fantasyland is based on fantasy and fairy tales. It has the most rides of any land in Magic Kingdom. Many Fantasyland rides feature classic Disney characters, such as Snow White and Dumbo. One popular ride is Mad Tea Party, in which visitors ride in spinning teacups during a tea party inspired by the film *Alice in Wonderland*. Another ride is Peter Pan's Flight, in which guests sit in cars suspended by rails. The cars make it feel as if riders are flying

Dedicated to the young, and young at heart, the many realms of fantasy that enchant across the resort promote the unabashed understanding that imagination is an important part of being.[8]

***—Kevin M. Kern, Tim O'Day, and Steven Vagnini, authors of* A Portrait of Walt Disney World**

On the Mad Tea Party ride, guests can make their teacup spin faster by turning a wheel in the center of the cup.

as they soar over animatronic figures and scenes of Neverland. Park guests can also take a trip through the Hundred Acre Wood on a ride called the Many Adventures of Winnie the Pooh. Fans of *The Little Mermaid* can enjoy scenes from the film on the Under the Sea ride.

Fantasyland is designed to look like a medieval European village, much like the ones featured in storybooks. Visitors can stroll through Belle's Village, a re-creation of the heroine's hometown in *Beauty and the Beast*. They can visit four castles: Cinderella Castle, Prince

Eric's Castle, Beast's Castle, and Rapunzel's tower. All of these were inspired by real European castles.

Fantasyland also features one of the only rides in the park that wasn't built by Disney Imagineers. It is called the Prince Charming Regal Carrousel. The carousel was built around 1917 and once belonged to an amusement park in New Jersey. It was shipped to Florida in 1967. Its 90 wooden horses were painted white because in fairy tales, most heroes ride white horses.[9]

CHAPTER
THREE

EPCOT

Since opening in October 1982, Walt Disney World's EPCOT has become one of the most visited theme parks in the world. Today, the park is a tribute to technological progress and world cultures. But originally, EPCOT wasn't meant to be a theme park at all—it was supposed to be a real city.

Walt Disney envisioned EPCOT as a utopian city where inventors, engineers, and artists would live and work together to build a better future. EPCOT is an acronym that stands for Experimental Prototype Community of Tomorrow. But during its development, the park was sometimes referred to as Progress City.

As Walt imagined it, the city would have a population of 20,000 people.[1] It would be

Walt Disney World has 12 monorail trains and three monorail lines. There are about 14.7 miles (24 km) of elevated monorail tracks throughout the entire park.

Don't Miss It!

Spaceship Earth

Spaceship Earth is a massive 180-foot- (55 m) tall sphere supported by six legs. It sits at the entrance of EPCOT, so it's the first thing visitors see when they enter the park. The sphere is made of more than 11,000 aluminum triangles. It's covered with 2,000 colorful lights that turn on at nighttime.[2] On special occasions, Imagineers add music and special effects to create a light show on the sphere's surface.

The sphere houses a ride called Spaceship Earth, which takes guests through the history of communication technology using detailed sets and audio-animatronics. Riders are taken back to the days of early humans painting on cave walls. Then they're pulled through time to witness the development of important inventions in history. Famous science fiction writer Ray Bradbury helped create the story for the ride.

laid out like a wheel, with neighborhoods surrounding a center hub of businesses. The entire city would be covered by a giant transparent dome, which would keep out rain and regulate the temperature. Instead of cars, mass public transportation in the form of monorails and PeopleMovers would take people where they needed to go. PeopleMovers are tram cars that move along tracks.

> **I often say that EPCOT is a park about people—the stories and curiosity that we share about our world, and the endless possibility that lives in each of us.**[3]
>
> *—Zach Riddley, Disney Imagineer, on EPCOT*

After Walt passed away in 1966, his company decided that building and running a city would be too difficult, and the project was put on the back burner for several years. In 1974, the company decided to move forward with a different vision of EPCOT. Instead of a city, EPCOT would become a theme park celebrating innovation and technology. Today, EPCOT is divided into four neighborhoods: World Celebration, World Nature, World Discovery, and World Showcase.

World Celebration

Visitors enter EPCOT through the World Celebration neighborhood. This neighborhood is full of attractions.

Some highlights include the iconic Spaceship Earth sphere and the Imagination! Pavilion.

The Imagination! Pavilion is housed in two giant glass pyramids. It's home to ImageWorks Labs, where guests of all ages can enjoy hands-on exhibits and games that spark imagination. The Pavilion also has a ride called Journey into Imagination with Figment. It takes visitors on a tour through sensory labs in the fictional Imagination Institute, where Dr. Nigel Channing attempts to show how the five senses play a role in imagination. But the tour is quickly taken over by Figment, a mischievous but lovable purple dragon.

World Nature

EPCOT's World Nature neighborhood celebrates the beauty and importance of the natural world. The neighborhood is split into two sections. These are called The Land and The Seas.

The Land building is home to greenhouses and two popular attractions. One is the Living with the Land ride. This boat ride carries visitors through a series of rooms that look like a rainforest, a desert, and a prairie. Visitors learn about each environment. They also see fruits and vegetables growing in greenhouses.

On the Living with the Land ride, guests cruise through a tropical greenhouse that has a large domed roof. A recorded voiceover tells guests about different environments, plants, and farming techniques.

The other attraction at The Land is called Soarin' Around the World. On this ride, park visitors can see what the world looks like from a bird's point of view. Riders board hang gliders that lift off the ground and tilt in front of a large movie screen. The screen shows scenes of natural wonders and famous sites around the world. The scenes were filmed using cameras mounted on airplanes and helicopters. The gliders move in a way that simulates the experience of soaring through the sky.

World Nature's second section is dedicated to the ocean. The Seas includes an attraction called The Seas with Nemo and Friends, in which visitors search for the lost clownfish from the 2003 film *Finding Nemo*. Guests board clamobiles, or cars shaped like clams. They enjoy a short underwater ride, during which animated sea creatures swim alongside more than 2,000 real creatures.[4]

Magic Agriculture

More than 30 short tons (27 metric tons) of fruits and vegetables are grown in EPCOT's greenhouses each year and served to guests at park restaurants. Some of the largest lemons in the world, weighing up to nine pounds (4 kg), were grown in The Land's greenhouses.[5] Visitors who look closely in the greenhouses might spot pumpkins and cucumbers shaped like Mickey Mouse. These are grown using special molds.

Visitors who prefer to stay above water can walk along the nature trail at Journey of Water. This attraction explores water's journey around the world and why the water cycle is important to the planet. It was inspired by the 2016 film *Moana*.

World Discovery

The third EPCOT neighborhood is World Discovery. It focuses on the wonders of outer space. Here, guests can find fan-favorite rides such as Guardians of the Galaxy: Cosmic Rewind and Mission: SPACE.

Cosmic Rewind was the first roller coaster built in EPCOT. Inspired by the *Guardians of the Galaxy* films, Cosmic Rewind invites guests into the Wonders of Xandar pavilion, which was built by Xandarians. These are fictional aliens from the films. In the ride, Xandarians have traveled to Earth from their home planet to teach Earthlings about their people, culture, and history. Then the Guardians of the Galaxy arrive to take guests on a pulse-pounding, high-speed intergalactic adventure.

Guardians of the Galaxy: Cosmic Rewind includes a pre-ride video featuring characters from the films. Huge screens are made to look like windows to outer space.

The Mission: SPACE attraction launches guests into a simulated journey through space, starting with a thrilling liftoff. Riders experience sensations that real astronauts experience when traveling in space, such as weightlessness. Guests can choose between two missions. One is an intense ride to Mars. The other is a calmer trip around Earth.

World Showcase

The largest neighborhood at EPCOT is World Showcase. It includes 11 pavilions that represent different countries around the world.[6] Each pavilion features exhibits, foods, entertainment, and replicas of famous buildings from the featured country. People who work at the pavilions are often from the country they're representing.

One pavilion features the North African country of Morocco. At the entrance to the Morocco pavilion, visitors can see a replica of the Koutoubia Minaret. This is a famous tower in the Moroccan city of Marrakesh. Moroccan artists helped build the pavilion and create the mosaic artwork featured inside it. The pavilion is designed to look like a bazaar, or marketplace. Its courtyard is filled with trees native to Morocco, including citrus, olive, date, and banana trees. Guests in the pavilion might spot a cast member dressed as Princess Jasmine from the film *Aladdin*.

A Real Blast!

Real astronauts and NASA scientists helped design Mission: SPACE to ensure the experience was accurate. The ride's designers used NASA satellite images of Mars's surface in the ride. They also modeled the attraction's "Ready Room" after Kennedy Space Center's White Room, where astronauts wait before boarding their spacecraft. When Mission: SPACE opened in 2003, some people found it a little too realistic. Designers had to make the ride milder. Mission: SPACE is the only Walt Disney World ride that provides emergency bags for motion sickness.

North America

World Showcase includes three North American countries. The Mexico pavilion features a massive pyramid based on the architecture of the ancient Maya and Aztec peoples. The pyramid is surrounded by a lush landscape designed to look like a Mexican jungle. Inside the pyramid is the Plaza de Los Amigos, which looks like a Mexican market, and a boat ride that takes guests past traditional Mexican architecture and a smoking volcano.

The United States pavilion is called American Adventure. It features Colonial-era architecture based on 1700s Philadelphia, Pennsylvania; Boston, Massachusetts; and Virginia. Guests can see a show called *The American Adventure*, which is hosted by audio-animatronic figures of Benjamin Franklin and American author Mark Twain.

The pyramid at the Mexico pavilion is modeled after the Temple of the Feathered Serpent, which is in the ancient city of Teotihuacán. The pyramid features serpent heads along its staircase.

The show discusses important events in US history. Visitors can also explore the American Heritage Gallery, which includes historical artifacts and artwork by American Indian artists.

The Canada pavilion features the Hotel du Canada, which is based on the famous Chateau Laurier in the country's capital city, Ottawa. The pavilion also has colorful gardens and a replica of the Canadian Rocky Mountains. The replica includes a 30-foot (9 m) waterfall.[7] The pavilion features a display of Indigenous inventions and artwork too. It includes totem poles, snowshoes, and kayaks.

Europe

Guests can explore several European countries at World Showcase. The Norway pavilion is modeled after an old Norwegian village. It features a 1200s wooden church and traditional houses with sod roofs. The church includes a gallery with real Viking artifacts. There is also a replica of a 1300s Norwegian fortress, which houses the Frozen Ever

A Trick of the Eye

Like Cinderella Castle, the American Adventure pavilion uses forced perspective. But the structure was designed to have the opposite effect. While forced perspective makes Cinderella Castle look taller than it really is, it makes the pavilion look shorter than it really is. This is to make the structure accurately reflect Colonial-era architecture, which features buildings that are never more than three stories tall. Imagineers made the bricks and windows toward the top of the pavilion larger than the ones toward the bottom. The building looks like it's only three stories, but it's actually five.[8]

The Frozen Ever After ride features audio-animatronics of *Frozen* characters, such as Queen Elsa. The audio-animatronics sing songs from the film.

After attraction. This is based on the 2013 film *Frozen*. Guests take a boat ride through the imaginary kingdom of Arendelle and Elsa's Ice Palace. Visitors are likely to run into cast members dressed as Anna and Elsa at this pavilion.

The Germany pavilion is designed to look like a plaza in a medieval Bavarian village. Bavaria is a state in Germany. One highlight at the pavilion is a fountain featuring a statue of Saint George slaying a dragon. Another is a clock tower. When the clock chimes on the hour, two mechanical figures pop out to ding the bell.

Lucky visitors might get a chance to meet Snow White at this pavilion.

The Italy pavilion was inspired by the Italian cities of Venice, Florence, and Rome. It features an 83-foot (25 m) replica of a bell tower from Saint Mark's Square in Venice.[9] Gondolas, boats often used as transportation in the canals of Venice, are moored nearby at a lagoon. To make the pavilion feel authentic, trees native to Italy are planted throughout the area. These include olive, citrus, kumquat, and cypress trees.

The France pavilion is modeled after a French village. It features a replica of the most iconic French landmark, the Eiffel Tower. The replica is about one-tenth the size of the real tower.[10] The pavilion is also home to Remy's Ratatouille Adventure, a 3D attraction based on the 2007 movie *Ratatouille*, which takes place in France. The ride is designed to make visitors feel as if they are the size of rats as they scurry through a fancy French restaurant. Guests can also meet a cast member dressed as Belle and enjoy a *Beauty and the Beast* sing-along show at the pavilion.

At the United Kingdom pavilion, visitors might feel as though they've been transported into the world of the film *Mary Poppins*—and they might even run into a cast member dressed as Mary Poppins. Some of the pavilion's architecture is inspired by the city of London. It features cobblestone streets and sooty chimneys. Other parts of the pavilion are modeled after an English countryside village with thatched-roof cottages. Visitors can also see replicas of England's iconic red telephone booths.

Asia

World Showcase includes two Asian countries. Visitors enter the China pavilion through an ornate, triple-arched ceremonial gate. The gate is a replica of one located at the Temple of Heaven in Beijing, China. After walking through the gate, visitors arrive at a replica of the temple itself. The pavilion is full of peaceful spots where guests can rest and enjoy natural features, such as waterfalls, ponds, and a bamboo garden. A cast member dressed as Mulan, the legendary Chinese heroine depicted in Disney's 1998 film *Mulan*, often appears at this pavilion.

At the Japan pavilion, guests can see a five-story, blue-roofed pagoda.[11] It is based on the Horyu-ji temple in Ikaruga, Japan. The pavilion also has gardens with bamboo groves and Japanese maple trees. The pavilion's White Heron Castle is modeled after a 1600s fortress. It houses a gallery of traditional and modern Japanese art.

The Temple of Heaven replica at the China pavilion is located next to ponds and a footbridge. The intricately detailed building lights up at night.

CHAPTER
FOUR

HOLLYWOOD STUDIOS

Disney's Hollywood Studios, originally known as Disney-MGM Studios, opened in May 1989. The park celebrates the magic of movies, television, animation, and filmmaking. It was designed to look like Hollywood, California—the birthplace of the US film industry—during the city's golden age. This was between the 1920s and the 1950s. Many buildings in the park are replicas of real buildings in Hollywood, such as the Carthay Circle Theatre. *Snow White and the Seven Dwarfs* debuted there in 1937.

The original purpose of Hollywood Studios was to give visitors a behind-the-scenes look at the film and television industries. It was meant to be both a theme park and a working

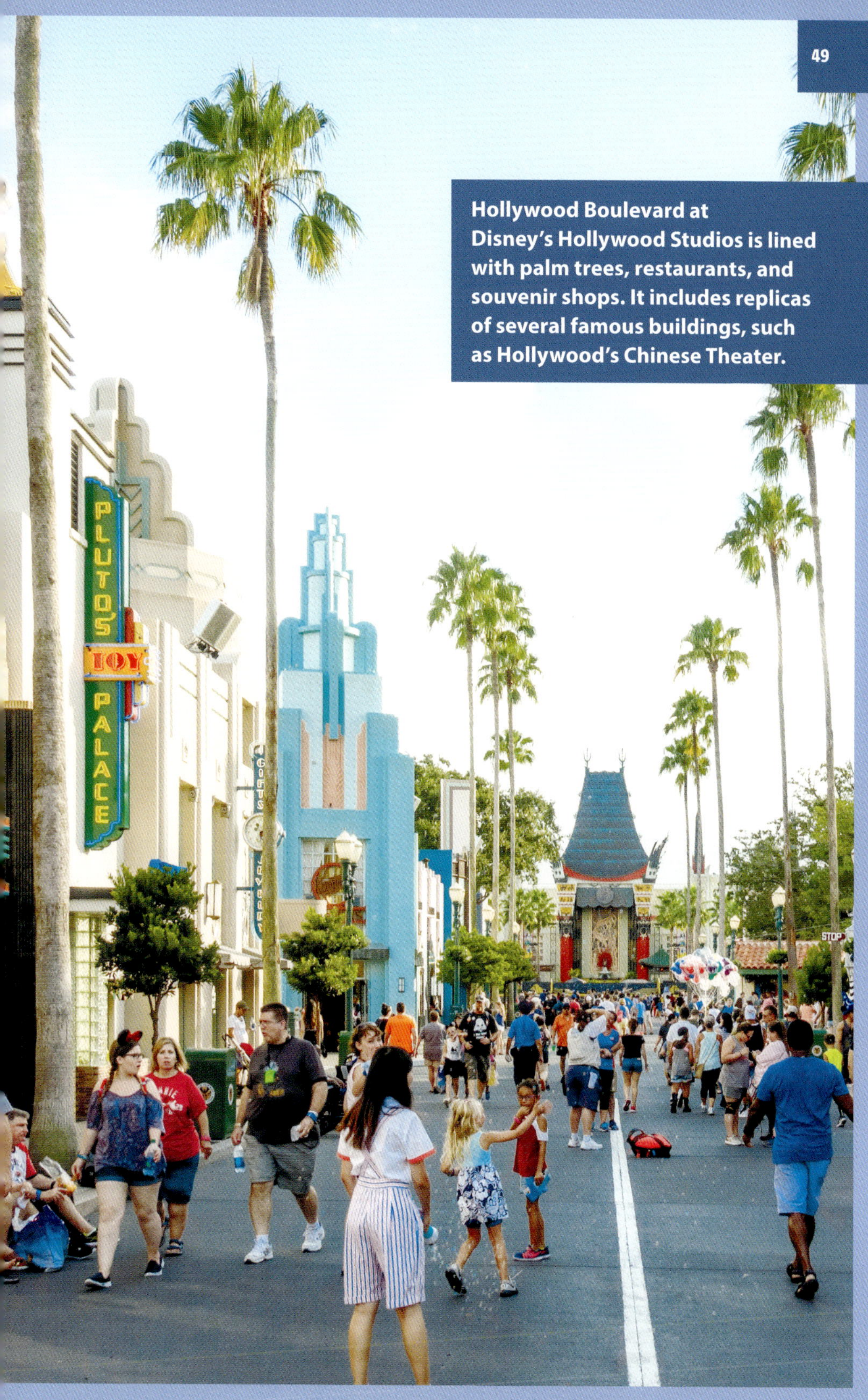

Hollywood Boulevard at Disney's Hollywood Studios is lined with palm trees, restaurants, and souvenir shops. It includes replicas of several famous buildings, such as Hollywood's Chinese Theater.

production studio. Some of the park's original rides included the Great Movie Ride, which took visitors on a journey through famous scenes of classic films, and the Backstage Studio Tour, in which guests learned about various aspects of film production.

The park also offered a behind-the-scenes tour of a real animation studio. The popular TV show *The Mickey Mouse Club* was filmed on-site at the production studio. Several celebrities, including actor Ryan Gosling and singer Britney Spears, got their start on the show. Over time, the vision for Hollywood Studios has changed. Today, instead of taking guests behind the scenes of movies, the park takes them into movies with immersive attractions and experiences.

> **"We are inviting our guests to step into these worlds of fantasy. It's no longer something you experience passively on a screen. It's living art, and you become the center of the story.[1]"**
>
> ***—Pam Rawlins, executive producer, Walt Disney Imagineering***

Hollywood Boulevard

Guests enter Hollywood Studios through Hollywood Boulevard. As they walk down this street, they may run into "streetmosphere" actors that add a sense of movie-industry atmosphere. These may include a young actress hoping to be discovered or an up-and-coming director looking for extras to be in his new film. These actors are meant to make the park feel like Hollywood.

Hollywood Boulevard is home to a ride called Mickey & Minnie's Runaway Railway. This was the first ride at any Disney park to feature Mickey Mouse and his friends. The ride takes guests through a movie screen and into a Mickey Mouse cartoon in which they're aboard a train driven by Goofy. Visitors zip through a wacky cartoon world where the rules of physics don't apply.

Echo Lake

Next to Hollywood Boulevard is an area called Echo Lake, which is inspired by the Echo Park neighborhood near Hollywood. Here, guests can find a wide range of attractions. One of the oldest is the *Indiana Jones Epic*

Read the Sign

To the left of the *Indiana Jones Epic Stunt Spectacular* entrance, visitors will find a well with a sign that reads "Warning! Do NOT pull rope." But "NOT" is crossed out on the sign. Visitors can pull the rope. Sometimes nothing happens when the rope is pulled. But often, the visitor will hear a recorded voice from inside the well yell, "Hey, what's going on up there?"[2] Other times, they will hear the scream of someone falling. Continuing to tug on the rope results in more responses.

The *Indiana Jones Epic Stunt Spectacular* features actors dressed as characters from the *Indiana Jones* films. One stunt in the show features an old-fashioned plane.

Stunt Spectacular. Inspired by the Indiana Jones film franchise, this live show features stunts like the ones seen in the movies. Stuntpeople act out scenes from the first Indiana Jones movie, *Raiders of the Lost Ark*. The show includes real fire, explosions, and other special effects. Then the stuntpeople explain how they did each stunt.

Another attraction in Echo Lake is Star Tours: The Adventures Continue. This ride is based on the *Star Wars* film franchise. It takes guests on a simulated journey through the galaxy. During the ride, guests watch a 3D movie featuring many characters from the *Star Wars* films.

There are about 50 different versions of the Star Tours ride.[3] Guests can ride it again and again and never know what to expect.

Animation Courtyard

Animation Courtyard was once a working studio where guests could get a behind-the-scenes look at the film industry. Today, it is home to a variety of attractions, including a special exhibit called Walt Disney Presents. This exhibit opened in 2001 to commemorate the hundredth anniversary of Walt's birthday. It features photos, sketches, costumes, and artifacts from Walt's life and work. After touring the gallery, visitors can watch a short documentary called *Walt Disney: One Man's Dream*. It includes audio recordings, historical film footage, and even some of Walt's home movies.

One artifact in the exhibit is the animation camera stand that Walt used to animate *Steamboat Willie*. This stand holds a camera that takes photos of the many drawings that make up an animated image. Other items include Walt's special Academy Award for *Snow White and the Seven Dwarfs* and his second-grade desk. If visitors look closely, they can spot where Walt carved his initials into the desk's surface.

Sunset Boulevard

Sunset Boulevard is another area of Hollywood Studios. It is named after a famous street in Hollywood. Here, park guests can find the Twilight Zone Tower of Terror ride, commonly called Tower of Terror. This attraction is inside the Hollywood Tower Hotel. At 199 feet (61 m) tall, the

At one point during the Twilight Zone Tower of Terror ride, the elevator doors open, giving riders a quick view of the park outside. Then the elevator plunges down again.

tower is one of the park's tallest attractions.[4] The ride is inspired by a popular TV show called *The Twilight Zone*, which aired from 1959 to 1964. Each episode featured a scary story with unexpected plot twists. The show was created and hosted by Rod Serling.

Guests start by walking through a dusty hotel lobby that seems frozen in time. The room is designed to look as though hotel guests have disappeared suddenly in the middle of the day. In the next room, a television turns on to reveal Serling, who welcomes the visitors. He explains that on Halloween night in 1939, lightning struck the hotel, causing a whole section of the building and an elevator carrying five people to disappear.

After learning about the hotel's history, riders take a seat in a big elevator. It takes them on a short tour of the hotel before the elevator cables "snap" and the elevator plunges down several floors. The elevator then shoots up

Pickled Pranks

Legend has it that the Imagineers who worked on the Tower of Terror liked to play pranks on each other. One prank involved Imagineers hiding in different spots and jumping out to scare each other with the same jar of pickled sausages. But someone accidentally left the jar behind on the night when all the ride's props were being glued down into place. Today, the jar still sits near the area where guests pick up their ride photos.

to the hotel's upper floors. The elevator plunges down several times at high speeds.

Another thrilling ride in Sunset Boulevard is Rock 'n' Roller Coaster. Guests ride in a car that looks like a stretch limousine. The roller coaster travels at high speed, going from zero to 60 miles per hour (97 kmh) in just three seconds, and it even flips riders upside down.[5] The ride features music by the rock band Aerosmith, which was popular when the ride opened in 1999.

Toy Story Land

Toy Story Land opened in Hollywood Studios in 2018. Here, guests have the chance to see the world from a toy's point of view. The area is designed to look like it was built by Andy, the young boy in the *Toy Story* films, in his backyard. It looks like it was made of typical items that a kid would have at his disposal, such as toy blocks and board game pieces. Giant items and structures make guests feel as though they've been shrunk down to the size of plastic toy soldiers. They follow a path of Andy's massive footprints.

The land is home to three *Toy Story*–inspired rides. Toy Story Mania takes guests inside a video game. After grabbing a pair of 3D glasses, guests board a car

Toy Story Land's Slinky Dog Dash roller coaster takes riders past giant statues of *Toy Story* characters, including Jessie and Rex.

and move through a series of five games. They use a spring-powered shooter attached to the car to hit moving targets. On the Slinky Dog Dash, visitors dash around Andy's backyard in cars shaped like the character Slinky Dog. On the Alien Swirling Saucers ride, guests hop into a spinning rocket-shaped toy pulled by a green alien.

Star Wars: Galaxy's Edge

In 2019, Walt Disney World opened Star Wars: Galaxy's Edge. This land is dedicated to the *Star Wars* film franchise.

Before boarding the Smugglers Run ride at Galaxy's Edge, riders walk through a full-size replica of the Millennium Falcon. The queue includes details from the *Star Wars* films.

After entering Galaxy's Edge, visitors find themselves on the fictional planet of Batuu. Although Batuu has never appeared in the *Star Wars* films, it is filled with architecture and landscapes similar to those in the movies. The land also features full-scale replicas of starships from the films, including Han Solo's Millennium Falcon and an X-wing Starfighter. There are many shops and restaurants in Galaxy's Edge too. At the Black Spire Outpost, guests can build their own custom lightsaber or droid. They can stop by Oga's Cantina for lunch.

Galaxy's Edge is home to two popular rides, Millennium Falcon: Smugglers Run and Star Wars: Rise of the Resistance. Smugglers Run takes guests on a wild ride in the cockpit of the Millennium Falcon as they attempt to deliver smuggled items. Rise of the Resistance combines several ride types, including a walk-through, buggy track, and simulator.

Guests find themselves launched into space aboard a transport shuttle. Riders are captured and taken prisoner by the villainous First Order. Then they must find a way to escape. Rise of the Resistance is one of the park's largest and most immersive attractions. It makes many visitors feel as if they're inside a *Star Wars* film.

Look and Listen

There is so much to see and do at Galaxy's Edge that it's easy for guests to miss the details. But guests should pay attention. If they listen closely while wandering through the street market or Resistance Forest, they'll hear the chatter of droids and Resistance fighters repairing their ships. If they look down, they'll see that the ground is covered in tracks left by Gungans—creatures from the planet Naboo—and droids.

CHAPTER FIVE

ANIMAL KINGDOM

On Earth Day, April 22, 1998, Walt Disney World opened its fourth park: Disney's Animal Kingdom. This park focuses on observing, appreciating, and protecting the natural world, and it includes a large number of live animals. Although Walt Disney didn't live to see the park himself, it was inspired by his dedication to animal conservation and the environment. Today, more than 13 million people visit the park annually, making it the most visited zoo in the world.[1]

Animal Kingdom is the largest of the four parks at Walt Disney World. It's also the world's largest theme park. Its 580 acres (235 ha) are home to more than 2,000 animals and 400 million plants.[2] The park was designed under the guidance

The Tree of Life is located in the center of Animal Kingdom. Visitors can go inside the tree's trunk to watch *It's Tough to Be a Bug!*, a 3D movie inspired by the film *A Bug's Life*.

of animal welfare specialists and conservation leaders. These experts continue to play an important role in caring for the park's animals and educating visitors about conservation.

Animal Tricks

When Imagineers were designing the Jungle Cruise in Magic Kingdom, Walt wanted to use real animals. Others cautioned against this because animals are unpredictable and hide when people are around. This was a concern at Animal Kingdom, too, so Imagineers came up with creative solutions to keep the park's animals visible. They do this by hiding water and food sources, such as salt licks and feeders, inside rocks and tree trunks. They also use temperature-regulated rocks that are heated in winter and cooled in summer to encourage animals to lie on them.

The Oasis and Discovery Island

After entering Animal Kingdom, visitors arrive at the Oasis. This area has no rides. It is a lush, tropical landscape with a small waterfall and a pond full of pink flamingos. At viewing areas around the landscape, lucky visitors might spot more animals that live in the Oasis. These include wallabies, tree kangaroos, two-toed sloths, colorful exotic birds, and a giant anteater.

After passing through the Oasis, guests cross a bridge to reach Discovery Island. This is the center of Animal Kingdom. It is connected to the rest of the park's areas by bridges. Discovery Island is home to the iconic Tree of Life. This tree has become the symbol of Animal Kingdom.

At first glance, the Tree of Life looks real. But it's actually made of concrete. The enormous human-made baobab tree is 145 feet (44 m) tall with a hollow trunk that is 50 feet (15 m) wide.[3] The trunk is so big that there's an entire movie theater inside it.

Welcome to a kingdom of animals . . . real, ancient, and imagined: . . . a kingdom we enter to share in the wonder, gaze at the beauty, thrill at the drama, and learn.[5]

—Michael Eisner, former Disney chief executive officer, in his 1998 dedication speech for Animal Kingdom

The tree's 8,000 branches are attached with joints so that they sway realistically in the wind. The branches are so strong that the tree can withstand hurricane-force winds. Artists created 325 animal carvings in the tree's trunk, roots, and branches. Some carvings are easy to spot from a distance, but visitors can get a close-up view by walking along the Discovery Island Trail.[4]

DinoLand, U.S.A.

Another area in Animal Kingdom is DinoLand, U.S.A. This land focuses on the dinosaurs and other prehistoric animals that roamed the planet millions of years ago. DinoLand doesn't take visitors back to the time of dinosaurs, though. Instead, it's designed to look like a worksite where paleontologists have unearthed dinosaur fossils.

One thrilling ride in DinoLand is called DINOSAUR. It takes guests back in time to the final minutes of the Cretaceous Period, the era in which the dinosaurs died out. Guests must rescue the last *Iguanodon* and bring it back to the present. Along the way, they must dodge fiery meteors and dinosaurs, including a *Carnotaurus* that is one of the largest audio-animatronic creatures that Disney has ever built.

DinoLand was scheduled to permanently close in 2025 to be replaced with a new land, Tropical Americas, in 2027. The new land will be modeled after the cultures and landscapes of Central America and South America. It will feature two new attractions. One will be an Indiana Jones ride that follows the famous character as he

David Greybeard

While artists were carving the Tree of Life, Jane Goodall—the world's leading expert on chimpanzees—was invited for a special viewing. Goodall asked the artists where they had carved the chimpanzee on the tree. They hadn't carved a chimpanzee and hadn't planned to. But after Goodall's visit, they changed their minds. The artists added a carving of David Greybeard to the trunk. He was one of Goodall's most famous chimpanzee subjects. David is the only named animal carved into the tree.

The queue for the DINOSAUR ride takes guests through the Dino Institute, where they can see a replica *T. rex* skeleton and other dinosaur bones.

explores a Maya temple. The other attraction will be a ride inspired by the magical house from the animated Disney film *Encanto*.

Asia

Two lands in Animal Kingdom are based on real places in the world. One is Asia. Guests enter Asia through the fictional kingdom of Anandapur, which means "place of delight" in Sanskrit. Anandapur was inspired by the architecture of rural communities in several South Asian countries, including Nepal, Cambodia, Thailand, and India.

Don't Miss It!

Expedition Everest

One of the most popular rides in Animal Kingdom is Expedition Everest: Legend of the Forbidden Mountain. This roller coaster is based on Mount Everest, the tallest mountain in the world. Everest is part of the Himalayan mountain range and is located between Nepal and Tibet.

The ride's queue leads visitors through the fictional Tibetan village of Serka Zong. Along the way, they pass the Yeti Mandir, a temple with shrines to the yeti. According to legend, this mythical apelike creature lives in the Himalayas. Visitors also pass through the Yeti Museum. Here, guests learn more about the yeti. They also learn about the Lost Expedition of 1982, a fictional group who went searching for the yeti and never returned.

Guests board a train that takes them on an exciting ride through dark caverns, forests, and snowcapped mountain peaks. After a steep ascent up the 199-foot- (61 m) mountain, guests discover that the track up ahead is broken and twisted. The train suddenly plummets backward into complete darkness, where a terrifying audio-animatronic yeti lurks. It stands 25 feet (8 m) tall.[6] Guests must race to escape the mountain before the yeti catches them.

The landscape is modeled after the jungles, rainforests, and foothills of the Himalayas, a mountain region.

Visitors can see several incredible animals in this area. The Maharajah Jungle Trek is a nature trail that winds through the Royal Anandapur Forest. It goes past the ruins of the Royal Hunting Palace of the Maharajahs, which has been reclaimed by nature. Along the trail, visitors can spot real animals native to Asia, including Komodo dragons, giant fruit bats, and tigers.

After a peaceful walk through the forest, guests can take a ride on the Kali River Rapids. They board a circular raft that floats freely in the river's current. Then they are carried through a dense rainforest past bamboo groves, waterfalls, and temple ruins. The ride ends with a heart-stopping plunge down a 20-foot (6 m) slope.[7]

Africa

The other Animal Kingdom land based on a real place is Africa. Guests arrive there through the rural East African town of Harambe, which means "let us all pull together" in Swahili. Like Anandapur, Harambe is a fictional place. But its architecture was inspired by a real island town called Lamu, which is located off the coast of Kenya. Every building in Harambe is a replica of a real building in Kenya, Zanzibar, South Africa, or another place in Africa. From the fortress to the thatched-roof huts, the buildings were based on real places Imagineers saw while traveling around the African continent. Many thatched roofs in the town were made by craftspeople from Zululand in South Africa.

In the Details

To ensure that the lands of Africa and Asia felt and looked authentic, Imagineers traveled around those continents for weeks while planning their designs for the park. They brought back items to place in exhibits and attractions around the lands. More than 2,000 authentic items throughout Expedition Everest were handcrafted in Asia.[8] This includes everyday items such as the nails used to hang pictures on the walls.

Guests have many opportunities to see animals in Africa. One of the most popular attractions in Animal Kingdom is the Kilimanjaro Safaris. This attraction was inspired by Lake Nakuru, a popular safari park in Kenya. Guests climb into safari-style jeeps for an 18-minute ride across the African savanna, where they can see animals native to Africa. These include hippos, giraffes, lions, zebras, and elephants.

This area of the park is designed to look as if the animals are roaming freely. But camouflaged fences and water features such as rivers and moats keep animals in their designated spaces. This keeps both the animals and guests safe.

Another attraction is the Gorilla Falls Exploration Trail, which goes through the Pangani Forest. On the trail, visitors may see grazing animals or spot hippos bathing in a watering hole. They may also see some gorillas.

Africa also provides guests with a unique opportunity to visit Rafiki's Planet Watch. The only way to get to this attraction is aboard a train called the Wildlife Express. The train takes guests to Conservation Station, where they can watch veterinarians treat animals or see experts prepare meals for animals. The park's animals eat an estimated 10,000 pounds (4,536 kg) of food every day.[9] Visitors can learn about ways to help animals and about conservation projects happening near their homes.

Kilimanjaro Safaris takes guests on a tour through the 110-acre (45 ha) Harambe Wildlife Reserve, which is home to more than 30 animal species.

Pandora: The World of Avatar

While most lands at Animal Kingdom are inspired by Earth's natural beauty, Pandora: The World of Avatar is unlike any place on Earth. It is based on an alien planet featured in the 2009 film *Avatar,* and it's the only place in the park that doesn't have live animals. The fictional planet of Pandora is home to floating mountains, glowing plants, and living beings called the Na'vi.

The Imagineers who designed Pandora wanted guests to feel like they were on another planet. They had to

At Pandora's Valley of Mo'ara, bridges and paths take guests past alien plants and waterfalls. Guests can even walk underneath the floating mountains.

figure out how to recreate the iconic floating mountains seen in the film. There are 22 floating mountains in Pandora's Valley of Mo'ara, and the tallest is about 130 feet (40 m) high.[10] Imagineers used steel beams camouflaged by limp vines to create the illusion that the mountains were floating. The bioluminescent plants were created using black-light paint and electricity. Hundreds of hidden speakers throughout the land play the sounds of both real and imaginary animals, giving the impression that the forests are full of creatures.

There are two popular rides in Pandora. One is Avatar Flight of Passage. On this simulator ride, guests put on 3D glasses and hop on motorcycle-like vehicles. The vehicles move in front of a movie screen, which makes it feel like guests are riding on Ikran, or mountain banshees. These fictional flying creatures look like dragons. Then guests soar over Pandora.

The other ride is the Na'vi River Journey. Riders travel down a river through a glowing rainforest full of exotic plants and creatures. In the depths of the rainforest, guests pass by a Na'vi called the Shaman of Songs, who is a gigantic audio-animatronic. After going on the rides, visitors can hike through the Valley of Mo'ara, where they'll find Na'vi instruments and totems along the paths.

CHAPTER
SIX

HIDDEN GEMS

For most people who visit Walt Disney World, the park's rides and attractions are at the top of their to-do lists. But Walt Disney World has much to offer beyond its rides, including live entertainment, interactive games, parades, and fireworks shows. It is also home to water parks, arcades, mini golf courses, a sports complex, and a massive shopping center. The park is full of hidden gems—visitors just need to know where to look.

Lesser-Known Attractions

With so many exciting rides at Walt Disney World parks, it's easy to miss some of the quieter attractions. One is Tom Sawyer Island in Frontierland, which can be reached only by raft. The island's name is

On the *Liberty Belle*, guests float past old-fashioned buildings on Tom Sawyer Island. During the ride, a recorded voiceover shares stories about Mark Twain's adventures on the Mississippi River.

a reference to *The Adventures of Tom Sawyer*, a novel by Mark Twain. It is about a boy named Tom living in Missouri in the 1840s. In the book, Tom travels down a river on a raft. There are no rides on the island, but visitors can explore suspension bridges, a working windmill, and three caves. They can stop and eat a picnic lunch on the island while enjoying the views.

Guests can also enjoy the view from the top of the Swiss Family Treehouse in Adventureland. This tree house is modeled after the one featured in the 1960 Disney film *Swiss Family Robinson*. In this movie, a family is stranded on an island, where they must battle pirates and survive other dangers. Visitors can freely explore the tree house's many rooms.

The Beloved Mr. Toad

Walt Disney World has changed a lot over the years, and sometimes old rides are removed to make space for new attractions. One of the most controversial changes was the removal of Mr. Toad's Wild Ride. This ride featured Mr. Toad, a character from Kenneth Grahame's 1908 novel *The Wind in the Willows*. In 1998, the ride was removed to make way for a new *Winnie the Pooh* ride. Mr. Toad's Wild Ride had been a beloved attraction in the park for 27 years.[1] People were so upset over its removal that they protested outside the park.

Another hidden gem in Adventureland is the Enchanted Tiki Room. Inspired by the culture and landscape of Polynesia, this attraction is a musical show featuring more than 225 audio-animatronic performers.[2] Many are tropical birds that sing and tell jokes. Others are flowers and totem poles.

The Liberty Square Riverboat is a quieter attraction. It features the *Liberty Belle*, a replica of the kind of steamboats that once took people up and down the Mississippi River. The boat's steam engine turns river water into steam, spinning the paddle wheel that makes the boat move. The *Liberty Belle* takes guests on a relaxing cruise around Tom Sawyer Island.

Scavenger Hunts, Missions, and Quests

Walt Disney World often invites guests to take an active role in adventures. One way the park does this is by offering free interactive games and quests. One example is A Pirate's Adventure, an interactive scavenger hunt in Adventureland. The goal of the hunt is to help Captain Jack Sparrow from *The Pirates of the Caribbean* films. Visitors must locate the Treasures of the Seven Seas while evading Sparrow's

> **These attractions are not merely our bodies being moved through sets, but our minds being moved between worlds, discovering everything anew.[3]**
>
> ***—Ridley Pearson, author, on Walt Disney World attractions***

enemies, such as Captain Barbossa and the Royal Navy. To join the hunt, guests visit a building called the Crow's Nest and pick up a talisman, which allows them to read a secret treasure map. Hunters complete one of five possible quests, each of which takes about 20 minutes.[4]

Visitors can do a similar scavenger hunt in EPCOT. It's called the DuckTales World Showcase Adventure. To play, guests download the Play Disney Parks app on their phones. They join Scrooge McDuck and his nephews from the animated show *DuckTales*, traveling around World Showcase to find seven lost treasures and return them to their owners. Missions take guests about 25 to 30 minutes to complete. There are seven missions to choose from, and each one takes place in a different country pavilion.[5]

At Animal Kingdom, nature enthusiasts can complete nature-themed challenges to become official Wilderness Explorers. This activity is inspired by the character Russell from the 2009 film *Up*. The challenges are self-guided. Participants may observe animals or learn wilderness skills.

Each time they complete a challenge, they earn a badge. There are more than 25 badges to collect.[6] To start, guests can pick up a handbook from the Wilderness Explorers headquarters or Troop Leader locations around Animal Kingdom.

Guests can use the Star Wars Datapad to unlock interactive experiences at Black Spire Outpost. They can scan hidden objects, intercept communication signals, and choose tasks from a job board.

Star Wars: Galaxy's Edge offers an interactive mission for both kids and adults. Guests can turn the Play Disney Parks mobile app into their own personal Star Wars Datapad. This includes all kinds of tools to help guests explore the planet of Batuu. It can be used to translate signs in alien languages or decrypt communications. It can also hack into or interact with devices, control panels, and droids. Guests can complete tasks for residents of Black Spire Outpost, members of the First Order, or members of the Resistance. When each

Off the Beaten Path

Hidden Mickeys

Hidden Mickeys are Mickey Mouse shapes hidden throughout rides, lands, and buildings within Walt Disney World. They started as an inside joke among Disney Imagineers in the 1980s. But today, finding Hidden Mickeys has become a game that delights guests of all ages.

There are at least 1,200 Hidden Mickeys throughout all four parks.[7] A complete list has never been made, so no one knows exactly how many Hidden Mickeys there are. People have even written books to help park visitors find as many Hidden Mickeys as possible.

Hidden Mickeys first started in EPCOT. Because this park doesn't feature fantastical characters like Magic Kingdom does, Imagineers had to get creative when incorporating Mickey into the park's design. As they worked, they found fun ways to include Mickey in the walls, floors, and artwork of the park's rides and attractions.

The Hidden Mickeys are usually just three circles. These represent Mickey's head and ears. Some are easy to spot, while others require some detective work.

In Magic Kingdom, Hidden Mickeys can be found in the African scene of the It's a Small World ride. Others are hidden on the stone seating area outside the Swiss Family Treehouse. The lock on the jail cell in the Pirates of the Caribbean ride is a Hidden Mickey too.

task is complete, players receive digital rewards, such as galactic credits or star maps.

Entertainment

Walt Disney World offers daily entertainment, including sing-alongs, story times, live performances based on classic Disney films, and even a comedy show. One of the most popular shows is *Fantasmic!* This nighttime musical takes place on Sunset Boulevard at Hollywood Studios. It is performed in an amphitheater by a lake. The 30-minute show includes fireworks, lights, music, special effects, and fan-favorite Disney characters.

The show tells the story of Mickey Mouse, who dreams that he's an apprentice to a sorcerer with the ability to control water, color, and magic. But Disney villains—including Maleficent, in the form of a 40-foot (12 m) dragon—turn Mickey's dream into a nightmare.[8] This results in a battle between good and evil. The show is so popular that people often arrive early to get a good seat.

At Hollywood Studios, guests can watch live performances based on two classic Disney films: *Beauty and the Beast* and *The Little Mermaid*. Both shows feature puppets and actors. They sing and act out the stories onstage. *Voyage of The Little Mermaid* includes special effects such as lightning strikes and mist to make the show feel more realistic. *For the First Time in Forever: A Frozen Sing-Along Celebration* also takes place at Hollywood Studios. It's located in the Hyperion Theater, where guests can watch parts of the film and sing along to their favorite songs. During the show, cast members dressed as Anna and Elsa appear live onstage.

At Animal Kingdom, two live shows take audiences into the worlds of the films *Finding Nemo* and *The Lion King*. *Finding Nemo: The Big Blue . . . and Beyond!* tells a

The *Festival of the Lion King* show features many songs from the film *The Lion King*, including "Hakuna Matata" and "Circle of Life."

story about Nemo. It includes catchy songs. Special lighting and effects make it feel as if the show is happening underwater. *Festival of the Lion King* is a musical show featuring the animals of the Pride Lands, who are holding a gala in honor of Simba. It features acrobats, enormous puppets, dancers in colorful costumes, and people walking on stilts.

A World of Entertainment

Guests can see exciting live performances at EPCOT's World Showcase, where many of the country pavilions feature entertainment from their country's culture. At the Mexico pavilion, guests can hear a mariachi band play Mexican folk music. Performers play traditional Bavarian folk tunes at the Germany pavilion. At the Japan pavilion, Japanese taiko drummers perform at the pagoda. An a cappella group called Voices of Liberty sings patriotic tunes at the American Adventure pavilion several times a day.

Magic Kingdom also offers shows. In Fantasyland, guests can watch *Mickey's PhilharMagic*, an animated 3D movie starring Donald Duck. The movie begins with Donald fast asleep, dreaming of putting on Mickey's sorcerer's hat. When he does, he's plunged into a world of musical scenes from classic animated Disney films.

Magic Kingdom is also home to the park's only comedy show, *Monsters, Inc. Laugh Floor.* This interactive show features monsters from the 2001 film *Monsters, Inc.* It is hosted by one of the movie's main monster characters, Mike Wazowski. Audience members can submit jokes before the show starts. Sometimes these jokes are used in the show.

Outside the Parks

Visitors can find lots of things to do outside Walt Disney World's four theme parks. Sports fans can check out the ESPN Wide World of Sports Complex. This sports facility is located south of the parks. It hosts thousands of events for athletes of all ages competing in more than 60 different sports.[9] Guests can stop by to watch a baseball game or soccer tournament. They must buy tickets ahead of time.

On days when the Florida weather is very hot, guests can cool off at one of Walt Disney World's two water parks. Blizzard Beach is a water park with a ski resort theme. It features a snow-covered mountain called Mount Gushmore. Typhoon Lagoon is designed to look as

Calling All Daredevils!

Blizzard Beach offers one of the most pulse-pounding attractions at Walt Disney World. The Summit Plummet waterslide is 360 feet (110 m) long with a nearly vertical drop.[10] Guests get on the slide via a platform that looks like a ski jump, which is 120 feet (37 m) in the air. Riders can reach speeds of up to 55 miles (89 km) per hour as they plummet 12 stories through a dark tunnel.[11] Summit Plummet is one of the tallest free-fall body slides in the world.

Blizzard Beach features multiple pools and waterslides. These include Summit Plummet, Cross Country Creek, and Downhill Double Dipper.

if a typhoon has swept through it, leaving a boat on top of a mountain in its wake. It is home to North America's largest wave pool, which generates waves up to six feet (2 m) high.[12] Both water parks have thrilling waterslides, raft rides, and pools to splash around in.

Guests can also explore Disney Springs, a large shopping center. It offers more than 90 stores and 70 restaurants.[13] Guests can check out giant statues made entirely of Legos. They can hitch a ride in an Amphicar, a car that floats on water like a boat. They can also go high up in the air in a tethered hot-air balloon.

CHAPTER SEVEN

HOTELS AND DINING

After a long day of thrilling rides and attractions, Walt Disney World visitors often need downtime. Luckily, there are more than 25 hotels at the park, so guests can rest and recharge without ever leaving. In fact, there are so many hotel rooms at Walt Disney World that a guest could stay in a different one each night for 68 years.[1]

Just like the different lands in the park, each hotel has a theme and offers unique experiences. Some guests spend the night at these hotels. Others visit to grab food at a hotel restaurant or check out some of the amenities.

Hotels at the Park

The closest hotel to Magic Kingdom was also one of the first hotels to open at Walt

At Walt Disney World's BoardWalk Inn, water taxis transport guests to and from the parks. At night, the hotel's boardwalk area is illuminated with strings of lights.

Guests at Animal Kingdom Lodge can book Savanna View rooms to get close-up looks at the hotel's wildlife.

Disney World: the Contemporary Resort. When it was built in 1971, the hotel looked very futuristic. It included talking elevators and a monorail that traveled right through the main building. To keep it true to its name, the Contemporary is regularly updated. In 2021, the hotel was updated to include artwork and characters from the superhero franchise *The Incredibles*.

Another hotel, located right across the water from the Contemporary, is a nature-lover's paradise. The Wilderness Lodge is surrounded by forests and nature trails. It is designed to look like a hotel at a national park in the Pacific Northwest. Guests can enjoy many fun outdoor activities at the nearby camping area, Fort Wilderness, even if they aren't staying overnight. Visitors can take archery lessons, rent a canoe, or hop on a horse and explore the trails.

One of the most unique hotels at Walt Disney World is the Animal Kingdom Lodge. It is inspired by the architecture of several lodges that Disney Imagineers visited while traveling around Africa. The hotel is surrounded by an animal reserve, which is modeled after an African savanna. It's home to more than 200 animals, including giraffes, zebras, flamingos, and gazelles.[2] Many of the hotel's rooms offer incredible views of the animals.

Walt Disney World hotels often make guests feel as though they've been transported to a different place. In fact, many of the hotels are inspired by specific places or eras, including New Orleans, Louisiana, and 1800s upstate New York. The Polynesian Village hotel features palm trees, a beach, and colorful buildings, making guests feel as if they're staying on a tropical island. It even has a pool with a fake volcano.

Star Wars: Galactic Starcruiser

In 2022, Walt Disney World opened a *Star Wars*–themed hotel called Star Wars: Galactic Starcruiser. The hotel was modeled after a *Star Wars* spaceship. It was also more than just a hotel. It was an immersive, three-day live-action role-playing experience. Guests were encouraged to dress up as *Star Wars* characters. They played a role in a storyline through interactions with cast members and through choices made via an app on their phones. Because it was expensive to stay at the hotel, few visitors could book the experience. The hotel closed less than two years after opening.

The BoardWalk Inn is designed to look like Atlantic City, a famous city in New Jersey. It has an old-fashioned boardwalk with games and food stands. It also has a carnival-themed pool area. The Coronado Springs Resort was inspired by the architecture of Mexico. Its pool features a 50-foot (15 m) replica of a Maya pyramid and a slide that passes beneath a water-spitting jaguar statue.[3]

Dining at Disney

At Walt Disney World, food is an important part of the experience. In fact, a whole team of chefs carefully designs every aspect of dining in the park. Walt Disney World includes more than 200 places to eat, from sit-down restaurants to food stands.[4] All four parks are home to restaurants with unique themes. These offer foods and experiences that visitors can get only at a Disney park, such as dining with cast members dressed as Disney characters.

Dinner and a Show

At some Walt Disney World restaurants, guests can enjoy live entertainment while they eat. One of the most well-known shows is *Hoop-Dee-Doo Musical Revue* at Pioneer Hall in Fort Wilderness. This is a two-hour comedy, dance, and music performance similar to shows that were popular during the early 1800s. Guests enjoy the show while chowing down on traditional barbecue foods such as fried chicken and cornbread.

Many treats at Walt Disney World, such as soft pretzels, waffles, ice cream bars, and beignets, are shaped like Mickey Mouse.

At Magic Kingdom, guests can find several fairy tale–inspired dining options. Two of the most popular restaurants are Cinderella's Royal Table and the Be Our Guest Restaurant. Both make visitors feel as though they've stepped into a storybook castle.

Cinderella's Royal Table is located inside Cinderella Castle. It has massive stone archways and stained glass windows, just like the castle in the film. Guests are likely to run into cast members dressed as Disney princesses while dining here. Cinderella herself often makes an appearance.

The Be Our Guest Restaurant is found at the foot of Beast's Castle in Fantasyland. It is inspired by the castle in the movie *Beauty and the Beast*. The restaurant is the only place in the park where guests can meet the Beast.

In Hollywood Studios, restaurants transport guests back to the golden age of Hollywood. The 50's Prime Time Café serves classic American comfort food in what feels like a real home kitchen from the 1950s. While they eat, diners can watch clips from popular 1950s TV shows on an old-fashioned TV set.

Another fan-favorite dining spot at Hollywood Studios is the Sci-Fi Dine-In Theater. Here, guests hop into car-shaped booths and eat while watching science fiction movie clips on a giant screen. The restaurant is designed to look like a 1950s drive-in movie theater.

EPCOT is home to a popular restaurant called Space 220. It is designed to look like a space station that can be reached only by riding a space elevator, or Stellarvator,

The car-shaped booths at the Sci-Fi Dine-In Theater feature illuminated taillights. Guests can order classic American food such as burgers and milkshakes.

Tasty Treats

All kinds of delicious treats can be found at Walt Disney World. But over the years, some snacks have become fan favorites. These include Mickey-shaped ice cream bars and giant turkey legs. One popular treat is Dole Whip, a pineapple-flavored soft-serve frozen dessert. Another is Grey Stuff, a mix of vanilla pudding, whipped cream, and chocolate cookie crumbs served on top of a cookie. Its name comes from a line in the song "Be Our Guest" from *Beauty and the Beast*. Lumiere, a talking candelabra, tells Belle to try the grey stuff.

220 miles (354 km) above Earth's surface.[5] The restaurant's windows are TV screens that show views of Earth in space, making guests feel as if they're really dining far above the planet. Guests can also spot spaceships and astronauts walking their dogs.

Many people consider EPCOT to be the best Disney park for foodies. This is because the park's food offerings are diverse. Each of the country pavilions sells traditional food and snacks from its featured country, so guests can taste food from all over the world just by walking from one end of World Showcase to another. They can grab lamb kebabs from Morocco, sushi from Japan, bratwurst from Germany, and crepes from France.

EPCOT also hosts a popular annual event called the EPCOT International Food and Wine Festival. During this event, guests can sample foods and drinks from around the world. They can enjoy special events and live entertainment too.

CHAPTER EIGHT

HOLIDAYS AND FESTIVALS

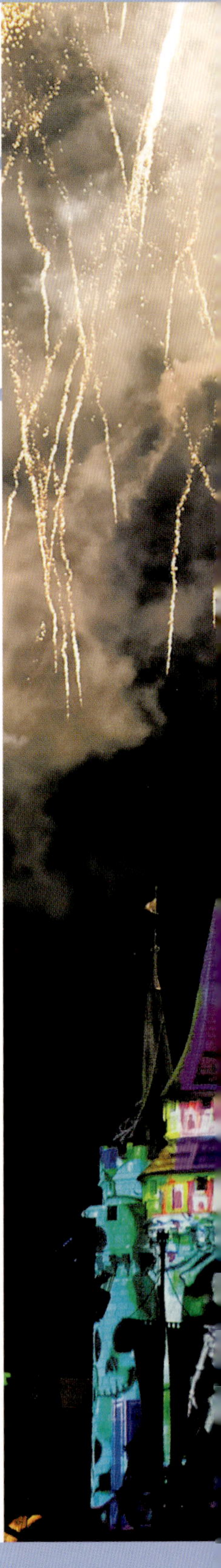

Many rides, attractions, and performances at Walt Disney World can be enjoyed year-round. But there are some events that visitors can experience only at certain times of the year. Many events are centered on specific holidays. These special events ensure that every visit to Walt Disney World, whether it's a guest's third or thirtieth visit, is a unique experience.

Walt Disney World's biggest holiday celebrations take place during Halloween and Christmas. If a guest were to visit Walt Disney World in October and December, the park would look quite different each time. That's because Walt Disney World gets a decorative makeover every Halloween and Christmas season.

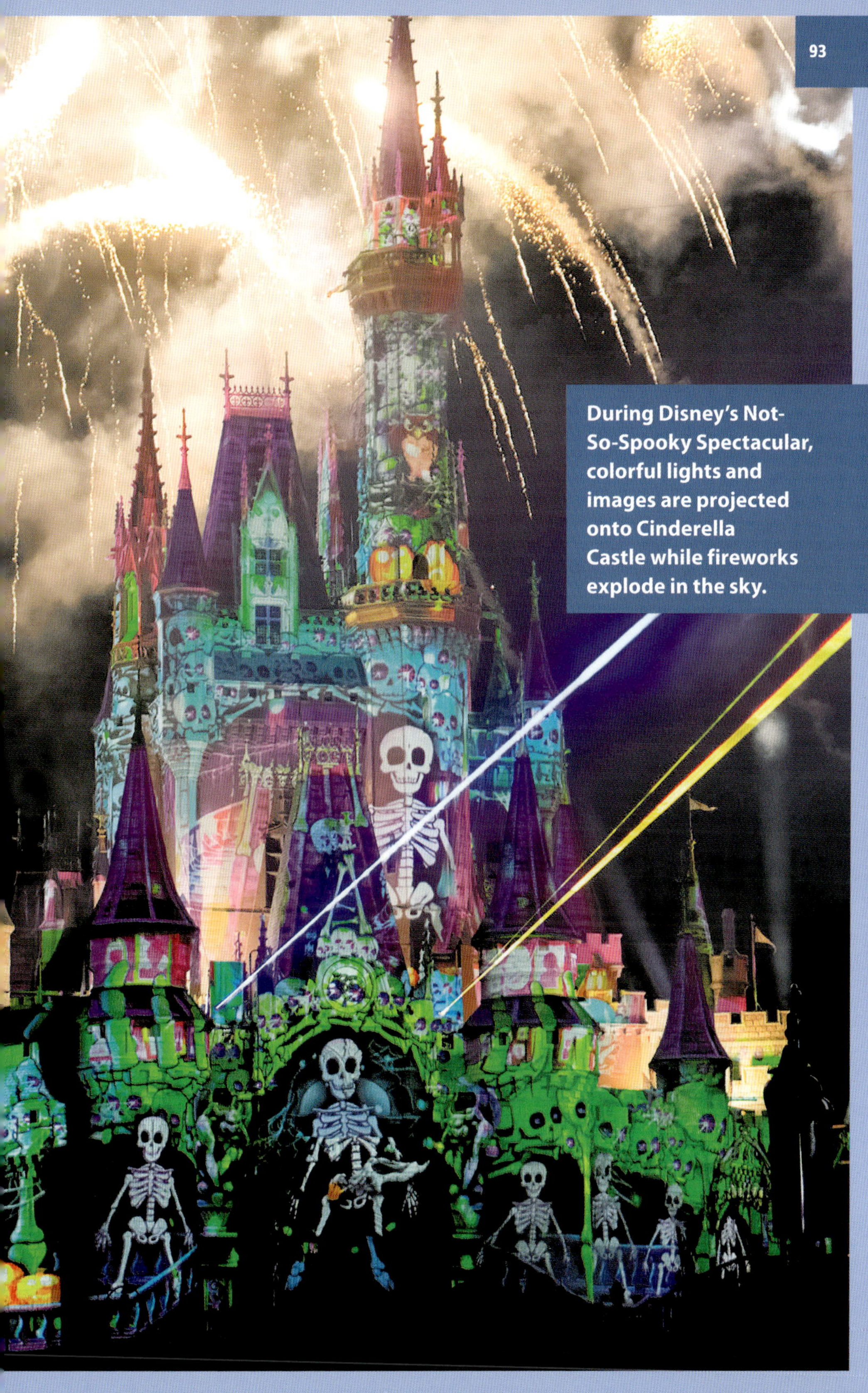

During Disney's Not-So-Spooky Spectacular, colorful lights and images are projected onto Cinderella Castle while fireworks explode in the sky.

Halloween

The Halloween season starts early at Walt Disney World, usually beginning in mid-August and lasting through October. Most Halloween-themed festivities, snacks, and souvenirs are at Magic Kingdom. Here, visitors can see Halloween decor, including jack-o'-lanterns, scarecrows, and orange-and-black banners. There are even Mickey-shaped pumpkin wreaths hung on lampposts along Main Street, U.S.A. Many rides and attractions, including the Mad Tea Party and Space Mountain, also receive special Halloween theming.

The main Halloween event at the park is Mickey's Not-So-Scary Halloween Party. This after-hours event features special entertainment, parades, and the chance to see beloved Disney characters dressed in their Halloween best. One highlight of the party is the *Hocus Pocus Villain Spelltacular.* This live stage show is hosted by the three Sanderson sisters, the villains of the 1993 film *Hocus Pocus*.

Earth Day at Disney

Earth Day, which is celebrated on April 22, is an important holiday at Animal Kingdom. Throughout the month of April, Animal Kingdom hosts special events and activities. These include drawing lessons with Disney animators. Guests learn how to draw Disney characters inspired by real animals. Guests have the opportunity to earn a special badge as a Wilderness Explorer too. They can also attend meet-and-greets with Disney characters, such as Baloo from *The Jungle Book*.

Guests can also see Disney's Not-So-Spooky Spectacular, a stunning nighttime laser, light, and fireworks show. During the show, Mickey and his friends find themselves trapped in a haunted house, where they encounter skeletons, ghosts, and a gang of Disney villains. Together, they must find a way to escape.

The Boo-to-You Halloween Parade is part of the festivities too. It features Mickey and Minnie dressed in Halloween costumes. The characters ride on spooky floats alongside familiar characters from the park's Haunted Mansion ride, such as the hitchhiking ghosts.

Christmas

Walt Disney World's biggest holiday celebration is Christmas. Christmastime at Walt Disney World begins in early November and continues through the end of the year. Unlike the park's Halloween festivities, which

It's a Jolly Holiday!

One special Christmas celebration at Walt Disney World is Jollywood Nights, which takes place at Hollywood Studios. This event includes several themed parties and shows throughout the park. Guests can watch a holiday show starring Disney characters and professional singers and dancers. Visitors can also gather around the park's Chinese Theater for Jingle Bell, Jingle BAM! This light and fireworks show includes clips of holiday scenes from Disney films, which are projected on the theater's exterior.

Christmas parades at Walt Disney World feature many holiday-themed floats and dancers. Cast members often appear wearing holiday costumes.

are largely limited to Magic Kingdom, Christmastime is celebrated in every land at Walt Disney World. Each land is decked out in special Christmas decor.

The main event is Mickey's Very Merry Christmas Party. Just like the park's Halloween party, this after-hours Christmas event features a parade, a fireworks display, and live entertainment. It also features special Christmas snacks and treats. During the event, guests can attend *Mickey's Most Merriest Celebration*, a stage production in which Mickey and other Disney characters sing holiday songs. Guests can also see Mickey's Once Upon a Christmas Parade, which features toy soldiers, gingerbread people, and a special appearance by Santa Claus.

Many rides get Christmas-themed makeovers with festive lights and holiday music.

EPCOT gets in on the holiday fun with its International Festival of the Holidays. During this festival, visitors can enjoy delicious holiday foods from around the world and learn more about winter holidays in other countries. International storytellers share information about holidays such as Hanukkah, Kwanzaa, and the Lunar New Year. Each country pavilion features its own holiday entertainment and special guests.

Running through the Park

Walt Disney World is known for its Halloween and Christmas celebrations, but fewer people know about the races and marathons held in the park each year. The park hosts several weekend-long running events. Many runners dress up as their favorite Disney characters or don tutus and tiaras for the event. The routes pass right through the parks, and participants receive medals when they complete the runs.

Other Festivals and Special Events

EPCOT hosts several other special events, including the International Festival of the Arts. This annual festival happens in January and February. It is centered on artists and art lovers. It features performances by world-renowned musicians, acrobats, and Broadway stars. There are live art demonstrations too. Guests can watch artists draw and paint Disney characters. The festival also offers many hands-on activities for young guests, including drawing lessons led by an animator.

Another EPCOT event is the International Flower and Garden Festival. In 2024, this took place from the end of February to the end of May. During this festival, visitors can admire detailed topiaries of Disney characters. The Japan pavilion features a dragon topiary that is nearly 20 feet (6 m) long.[1] Visitors can also explore fascinating garden exhibits. One is the floating gardens at World Nature, where flowers float on a pond's surface. Another is the Prehistoric Garden, which features plants that have existed on Earth since the time of dinosaurs 65 million years ago.

A Place of Magic

Walt Disney World has changed a lot over the years. When it first opened in 1971, it consisted of just one park with only 26 attractions.[2] Today, it has four parks with more than 170 attractions.[3] The park has also expanded to include two water parks, more than 25 hotels, more than 200 places to eat, and hundreds of stores.[4] With so much growth, it's no wonder Walt Disney World is the most visited theme park in the world. But one thing that hasn't changed is the park's ability to transport guests to a place where anything feels possible.

> **It's a place where, no matter how old you are, you feel that same childlike awe and excitement.**[5]
> ***—Bob Chapek, CEO of Disney, on Walt Disney World***

In 2023, Walt Disney World opened Dreamer's Point, a sitting area in EPCOT's World Celebration. The quiet spot is surrounded by beautiful gardens and features a statue of Walt Disney titled *Walt the Dreamer*. Although park visitors will never have the chance to meet Walt in person, they can sit down beside him for a while and consider the magic of the place he helped create—even if he never set foot in the park himself.

In 2023, one set of topiaries at EPCOT's International Flower and Garden Festival showcased the classic characters Mickey, Minnie, Pluto, Chip, and Dale.

ESSENTIAL FACTS

WALT DISNEY WORLD BASICS

- Walt Disney World is a theme park inspired by the imaginative ideas and designs of Walt Disney.
- Walt Disney World is the world's largest theme park and consists of four lands. These are Magic Kingdom, EPCOT, Hollywood Studios, and Animal Kingdom.
- Walt Disney World opened on October 1, 1971. It is located in central Florida, near the city of Orlando.
- Walt Disney World is the most visited theme park in the world, with more than 58 million visitors annually.
- Walt Disney World is home to more than 170 attractions. It includes two water parks, more than 25 hotels, more than 200 places to eat, and hundreds of stores.

THINGS TO SEE AND DO

- Ride a Doom Buggy through the Haunted Mansion in Magic Kingdom's Liberty Square.
- Visit Magic Kingdom's Adventureland and experience scenes of pirate life on the Pirates of the Caribbean ride.
- Explore the world of *Star Wars* at Star Wars: Galaxy's Edge in Hollywood Studios and experience the immersive Rise of the Resistance attraction.
- Celebrate Halloween with parades, activities, and more during Mickey's Not-So-Scary Halloween Party.
- Sample foods and drinks from around the world at the EPCOT International Food and Wine Festival.
- Take a ride through the mysterious Forbidden Mountain on the Expedition Everest roller coaster at Animal Kingdom.

MAP

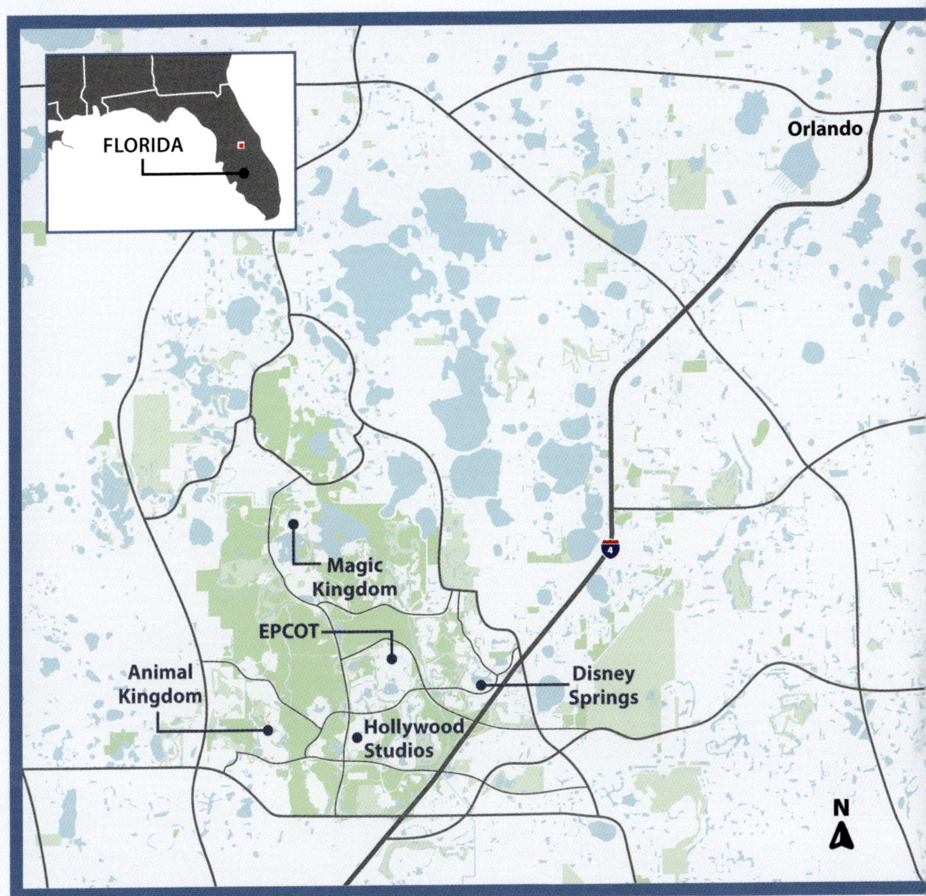

QUOTE

"We are inviting our guests to step into these worlds of fantasy. It's no longer something you experience passively on a screen. It's living art, and you become the center of the story."

—Pam Rawlins, executive producer,
Walt Disney Imagineering

GLOSSARY

amenity

A feature of a place, such as a hotel, that provides comfort, entertainment, or convenience.

amphitheater

An open, circular building with a central stage surrounded by seating where an event such as a performance occurs.

animator

An artist who helps create animated cartoons or films.

bioluminescent

Describing a living organism that has the ability to emit bright, colorful light.

franchise

A series of films, as well as other associated media, that share a setting, a story, or characters.

frontier

A region on the border of settled territory, where unexplored, unsettled land begins.

innovative

Having original or creative ideas.

monorail

A track that consists of a single, usually elevated rail along which a vehicle travels.

paleontologist

Someone who studies dinosaurs or other life from previous geologic periods.

pavilion

A large, open building or a group of buildings with an open area in the middle.

prosperous

Thriving or demonstrating health and wealth.

prototype

A first or typical model for something.

queue

A line for a ride.

simulated

Made to look, seem, or feel real.

topiary

A tree or shrub cut into a decorative shape.

utopian

Having the qualities of a place that is considered ideal or perfect.

ADDITIONAL RESOURCES

SELECTED BIBLIOGRAPHY

Brandon, Pam. *Delicious Disney: Walt Disney World*. Disney Editions, 2021.

Kern, Kevin M., Tim O'Day, and Steven Vagnini. *A Portrait of Walt Disney World: 50 Years of the Most Magical Place on Earth*. Disney Editions, 2021.

Veness, Susan. *The Hidden Magic of Walt Disney World*. 3rd ed., Adams Media, 2020.

FURTHER READINGS

Birnbaum's Walt Disney World: The Official Vacation Guide 2025. Disney Editions, 2024.

Kallen, Stuart A. *Exploring Animation*. ReferencePoint, 2025.

Murray, Laura K. *The Movie Encyclopedia*. Abdo, 2024.

ONLINE RESOURCES

To learn more about Walt Disney World, please visit **abdobooklinks.com** or scan this QR code. These links are routinely monitored and updated to provide the most current information available.

MORE INFORMATION

For more information on this subject, contact or visit the following organizations:

THE WALT DISNEY FAMILY MUSEUM

104 Montgomery St.
San Francisco, CA 94129
waltdisney.org

The Walt Disney Family Museum focuses on the life and work of Walt Disney. It houses hundreds of historical documents and artifacts related to Walt and his work.

WALT DISNEY HOMETOWN MUSEUM

120 E. Santa Fe Ave.
Marceline, MO 64658
waltdisneymuseum.org

The Walt Disney Hometown Museum was originally built around the personal collection of Walt Disney's sister, Ruth. It houses more than 4,000 artifacts related to Walt, including personal letters and photos.

WALT DISNEY WORLD: MAGIC KINGDOM PARK

1180 Seven Seas Dr.
Lake Buena Vista, FL 32830
disneyworld.disney.go.com/destinations/magic-kingdom

Walt Disney World's Magic Kingdom is home to themed lands, popular attractions, and classic rides. Guests can also visit the Guest Relations Lobby in Main Street, U.S.A.'s City Hall. Here, they can find park maps, ask questions, and learn more about the park.

SOURCE NOTES

CHAPTER 1. THE HISTORY OF WALT DISNEY WORLD

1. Rick Bragg. "Disney World." *Tampa Bay Times*, 13 Oct. 2005, tampabay.com. Accessed 17 Dec. 2024.
2. Stephen Vagnini. "How Walt Disney World Found Its Home in Florida." *D23*, 28 Sept. 2016, d23.com. Accessed 17 Dec. 2024.
3. Aaron H. Goldberg. *Buying Disney's World*. Quaker Scribe, 2021. 62.
4. Ian Webster. "Value of $145 from 1964 to 2024." *CPI Inflation Calculator*, n.d., in2013dollars.com. Accessed 19 Dec. 2024.
5. Goldberg, *Buying Disney's World*, 92.
6. Ian Webster. "Value of $1,000 from 1965 to 2024." *CPI Inflation Calculator*, n.d., in2013dollars.com. Accessed 19 Dec. 2024.
7. Goldberg, *Buying Disney's World*, 78.
8. "Walt Disney's E.P.C.O.T Film (1966)." *YouTube*, uploaded by The Original EPCOT, 23 Sept. 2013, youtube.com.
9. "Honorary Academy Award." *Walt Disney Family Museum*, 23 Feb. 2023, waltdisney.org. Accessed 8 Jan. 2025.
10. Aliza Chasan. "Who Has the Most Oscars of All Time?" *CBS News*, 11 Mar. 2024, cbsnews.com. Accessed 19 Dec. 2024.
11. "Reinventing the American Amusement Park." *PBS: American Experience*, n.d., pbs.org. Accessed 19 Dec. 2024.
12. Kevin M. Kern, Tim O'Day, and Steven Vagnini. *A Portrait of Walt Disney World*. Disney Editions, 2021. 22.
13. Rudie Obias. "Disneyland vs. Disney World." *Reader's Digest*, 19 June 2024, rd.com. Accessed 19 Dec. 2024.
14. Greg Allen. "50 Years Ago, Disney World Opened Its Doors." *NPR*, 1 Oct. 2021, npr.org. Accessed 19 Dec. 2024.
15. "Sustainable Tourism." *Mouse Experts*, n.d., themouseexperts.com. Accessed 19 Dec. 2024.
16. Goldberg, *Buying Disney's World*, 159.
17. Allen, "Disney World Opened Its Doors."
18. Ian Webster. "Value of $400,000,000 from 1971 to 2024." *CPI Inflation Calculator*, n.d., in2013dollars.com. Accessed 19 Dec. 2024.
19. "Walt Disney World Statistics." *Magic Guides*, n.d., magicguides.com. Accessed 19 Dec. 2024.
20. Amanda Krause. "Disney World Iconic Entrance." *Business Insider*, 27 Oct. 2020, businessinsider.com. Accessed 19 Dec. 2024.

CHAPTER 2. MAGIC KINGDOM

1. Jeff Bogle. "Disney World's Cinderella Castle." *Reader's Digest*, 20 Sept. 2024, rd.com. Accessed 19 Dec. 2024.
2. Bogle, "Disney World's Cinderella Castle."

3. Caitlin Kane. "Main Street, U.S.A." *Disney Dining*, 22 Dec. 2021, disneydining.com. Accessed 19 Dec. 2024.

4. Susan Veness. *The Hidden Magic of Walt Disney World*. 3rd ed., Adams Media, 2020. 17.

5. Brooks Barnes. "Are You Ready for Sentient Disney Robots?" *New York Times*, 19 Aug. 2021, nytimes.com. Accessed 19 Dec. 2024.

6. "Tiana's Bayou Adventure." *Walt Disney World*, n.d., disneyworld.disney.go.com. Accessed 19 Dec. 2024.

7. "Space Mountain." *D23*, n.d., d23.com. Accessed 19 Dec. 2024.

8. Kevin M. Kern, Tim O'Day, and Steven Vagnini. *A Portrait of Walt Disney World*. Disney Editions, 2021. 77.

9. "Prince Charming Regal Carrousel." *Walt Disney World*, n.d., disneyworld.disney.go.com. Accessed 19 Dec. 2024.

CHAPTER 3. EPCOT

1. Kirsten Acuna. "Walt Disney's Original Plan for Epcot." *Business Insider*, 26 June 2012, businessinsider.com. Accessed 19 Dec. 2024.

2. Karyn Locke. "EPCOT's Spaceship Earth." *WDW Magazine*, 5 Apr. 2023, wdw-magazine.com. Accessed 19 Dec. 2024.

3. "Update on EPCOT's 'Journey of Water.'" *WDW Magic*, 5 May 2022, wdwmagic.com. Accessed 30 Dec. 2024.

4. "The Seas with Nemo & Friends." *Guide to the Magic*, n.d., guidetothemagic.com. Accessed 19 Dec. 2024.

5. Christy Lynch. "How Walt Disney World's Farm Grows Produce." *Farm Flavor*, 2 Mar. 2018, farmflavor.com. Accessed 19 Dec. 2024.

6. Jenn Marrazzo. "Secret Details in World Showcase." *WDW Magazine*, 6 Aug. 2024, wdw-magazine.com. Accessed 19 Dec. 2024.

7. "Canada Pavilion." *AllEars*, n.d., allears.net. Accessed 19 Dec. 2024.

8. Tim Foster. "Seven Things about the American Adventure." *Celebrations Press*, 3 July 2017, celebrationspress.com. Accessed 19 Dec. 2024.

9. Emily Owens Pickle. "Italy vs 'Italy' Epcot." *AllEars*, 3 Aug. 2010, allears.net. Accessed 19 Dec. 2024.

10. Scott Thomas. "Epcot's Eiffel Tower." *AllEars*, 8 Dec. 2011, allears.net. Accessed 19 Dec. 2024.

11. "Japan." *AllEars*, n.d., allears.net. Accessed 19 Dec. 2024.

CHAPTER 4. HOLLYWOOD STUDIOS

1. Kevin M. Kern, Tim O'Day, and Steven Vagnini. *A Portrait of Walt Disney World*. Disney Editions, 2021. 133.

SOURCE NOTES CONTINUED

2. Jim Korkis. *Final Secret Stories of Walt Disney World*. Theme Park Press, 2022. 65–66.

3. "Star Tours." *Mouse for Less*, n.d., themouseforless.com. Accessed 19 Dec. 2024.

4. "Twilight Zone Tower of Terror Ultimate Guide." *AllEars*, n.d., allears.net. Accessed 19 Dec. 2024.

5. "Rock 'n' Roller Coaster Starring Aerosmith." *AllEars*, n.d., allears.net. Accessed 19 Dec. 2024.

CHAPTER 5. ANIMAL KINGDOM

1. "Most Visited Zoo (Current)." *Guinness World Records*, n.d., guinnessworldrecords.com. Accessed 19 Dec. 2024.

2. "Guide to Visiting Disney's Animal Kingdom." *Moms with Mouse Ears*, n.d., momswithmouseears.com. Accessed 19 Dec. 2024.

3. Karyn Locke. "6 Fun Facts about the Tree of Life." *WDW Magazine*, 13 Apr. 2020, wdw-magazine.com. Accessed 20 Dec. 2024.

4. Locke, "6 Fun Facts about the Tree of Life."

5. Blake Taylor. "1998's Animal Kingdom Dedication." *Attractions Magazine*, 19 Apr. 2023, attractionsmagazine.com. Accessed 20 Dec. 2024.

6. Jim Korkis. "Yeti and the Forbidden Mountain." *MousePlanet*, 3 Feb. 2021, mouseplanet.com. Accessed 20 Dec. 2024.

7. "Kali River Rapids." *Walt Disney World*, n.d., disneyworld.disney.go.com. Accessed 20 Dec. 2024.

8. Tim Foster. "Six Things about Expedition Everest." *Celebrations Press*, 29 July 2018, celebrationspress.com. Accessed 20 Dec. 2024.

9. Dr. Mark Penning. "Conservation & Animal Care." *Disney Parks Blog*, 22 Apr. 2024, disneyparksblog.com. Accessed 20 Dec. 2024.

10. Steve Spears. "Animal Kingdom 25th Anniversary." *Florida Travel + Life*, 21 Apr. 2023, floridatravellife.com. Accessed 20 Dec. 2024.

CHAPTER 6. HIDDEN GEMS

1. "Toad's 27-Year Ride Ends." *Washington Post*, 3 Sept. 1998, washingtonpost.com. Accessed 20 Dec. 2024.

2. "Walt Disney's Enchanted Tiki Room." *Walt Disney World*, n.d., disneyworld.disney.go.com. Accessed 20 Dec. 2024.

3. Kevin M. Kern, Tim O'Day, and Steven Vagnini. *A Portrait of Walt Disney World*. Disney Editions, 2021. 158.

4. "A Pirate's Adventure." *Walt Disney World*, n.d., disneyworld.disney.go.com. Accessed 20 Dec. 2024.

5. Kaitlyn Killebrew. "DuckTales World Showcase Adventure." *Visit Orlando*, 2 Jan. 2023, bestoforlando.com. Accessed 20 Dec. 2024.

6. "Wilderness Explorers." *Walt Disney World*, n.d., disneyworld.disney.go.com. Accessed 20 Dec. 2024.

7. Alyssa Spagna. "Hidden Mickeys at Disney World." *Jetset Times*, 23 Feb. 2023, jetsettimes.com. Accessed 20 Dec. 2024.

8. "Fantasmic!" *Walt Disney World*, n.d., disneyworld.disney.go.com. Accessed 20 Dec. 2024.

9. Heather Adams. "ESPN Wide World of Sports." *WDW Magazine*, 28 Feb. 2024, wdw-magazine.com. Accessed 20 Dec. 2024.

10. "Summit Plummet." *Walt Disney World*, n.d., disneyworld.disney.go.com. Accessed 20 Dec. 2024.

11. "Summit Plummet." *Enjoy Florida Online*, n.d., enjoyflorida.com. Accessed 20 Dec. 2024.

12. "Typhoon Lagoon Surf Pool." *Walt Disney World*, n.d., disneyworld.disney.go.com. Accessed 20 Dec. 2024.

13. "Disney Springs." *Disney Springs*, n.d., disneysprings.com. Accessed 20 Dec. 2024.

CHAPTER 7. HOTELS AND DINING

1. Melissa Cannioto. "Astonishing Disney Hotel Room Fact." *Disney Tips*, 16 June 2022, disneytips.com. Accessed 20 Dec. 2024.

2. "Disney's Animal Kingdom Lodge." *Walt Disney World*, n.d., disneyworld.disney.go.com. Accessed 20 Dec. 2024.

3. "Disney's Coronado Springs Resort." *Walt Disney World*, n.d., disneyworld.disney.go.com. Accessed 20 Dec. 2024.

4. Heather Adams. "Walt Disney World Dining." *WDW Magazine*, 6 Mar. 2024, wdw-magazine.com. Accessed 20 Dec. 2024.

5. "Space 220 Restaurant." *Walt Disney World*, n.d., disneyworld.disney.go.com. Accessed 20 Dec. 2024.

CHAPTER 8. HOLIDAYS AND FESTIVALS

1. "2025 EPCOT Flower and Garden Festival." *Mouse for Less*, n.d., themouseforless.com. Accessed 20 Dec. 2024.

2. "Walt Disney World Statistics." *Magic Guides*, n.d., magicguides.com. Accessed 19 Dec. 2024.

3. Natalie Cheese. "Guide to Rides at Disney World." *Top Villas*, n.d., thetopvillas.com. Accessed 19 Dec. 2024.

4. "Walt Disney World Statistics."

5. Kevin M. Kern, Tim O'Day, and Steven Vagnini. *A Portrait of Walt Disney World*. Disney Editions, 2021. 8.

INDEX

Academy Awards, 9–10, 53
American Revolutionary War, 20–21
Animal Kingdom, 60–71, 76, 80–81, 87, 94
  Africa, 67–69
  Asia, 65–67, 68
  DinoLand, U.S.A., 63–64
  Discovery Island, 62–63
  Oasis, the, 62
  Pandora: The World of Avatar, 70–71
  Tropical Americas, 64–65
audio-animatronics, 21–22, 23, 25, 26, 28, 30, 34, 41, 64, 66, 71, 75

Beauty and the Beast, 30–31, 45, 79, 89, 91
Big Thunder Mountain Railroad, 24
Blizzard Beach, 82

Christmas, 92, 95–97
  International Festival of the Holidays, 97
  Jollywood Nights, 95
  Mickey's Very Merry Christmas Party, 96–97
Cinderella Castle, 16, 18, 30–31, 43, 89
conservation, 60, 62, 69

Disney, Roy, 4–9, 14–15
Disney, Walt, 4–10, 12–15, 19–20, 23, 27, 32, 35, 53, 60, 62, 99
Disney Springs, 83
Disneyland, 10–13, 29

Enchanted Tiki Room, 74–75
EPCOT, 32–46, 76, 78, 81, 90–91, 97–98, 99
  World Celebration, 35–36, 99
  World Discovery, 35, 38–40
  World Nature, 35, 36–38, 98
  World Showcase, 35, 40–46, 76, 81, 91
EPCOT International Food and Wine Festival, 91
ESPN Wide World of Sports Complex, 82
Expedition Everest, 66, 68

Fantasmic!, 79
Finding Nemo, 38, 80–81
Frozen, 43–44, 80

Guardians of the Galaxy: Cosmic Rewind, 38–39

Hall of Presidents, 21–22
Halloween, 55, 92–96, 97
  Mickey's Not-So-Scary Halloween Party, 94–95
Haunted Mansion, 22–23, 26, 95
Hollywood Studios, 48–59, 79–80, 90, 95
  Animation Courtyard, 53
  Echo Lake, 51–53
  Hollywood Boulevard, 50–51
  Star Wars: Galaxy's Edge, 57–59, 77, 79
  Sunset Boulevard, 54–56, 79
  Toy Story Land, 56–57
hotels, 12–13, 43, 54–56, 84–88, 98

Imagineers, 23, 31, 34, 35, 43, 50, 55, 62, 68, 70–71, 78, 87
Indiana Jones, 51–52, 64–65
International Festival of the Arts, 97–98
International Flower and Garden Festival, 98

Jungle Cruise, 25–26, 62

Little Mermaid, The, 30, 79–80
live shows, 52, 72, 79–82, 88, 91, 94, 96

Mad Tea Party, 29, 94
Magic Kingdom, 16–31, 62, 78, 81, 84, 89, 94, 96
  Adventureland, 16, 25–26, 74–76
  Fantasyland, 16, 29–31, 81, 89
  Frontierland, 16, 23–25, 72–75
  Liberty Square, 16, 20–23, 75
  Main Street, U.S.A., 16, 19–20, 21, 26, 94
  Tomorrowland, 16, 27–29
Marceline, Missouri, 7, 19
Mickey Mouse, 9, 38, 50, 51, 78, 79, 81, 91, 94–95, 96
  Hidden Mickeys, 78
Millennium Falcon: Smugglers Run, 59
Mission: SPACE, 38, 40, 41
monorails, 35, 86

Orlando Sentinel, 6

PeopleMovers, 35
Peter Pan's Flight, 29–30
Pirates of the Caribbean, 26, 75, 78

restaurants, 12, 16, 19, 38, 45, 58, 83, 84, 88–91

scavenger hunts, 75–76
shops, 12, 16, 19–20, 21, 23, 58, 72, 83, 98
Snow White and the Seven Dwarfs, 9, 29, 45, 48, 53
Space Mountain, 28–29, 94
Spaceship Earth, 34, 36
Star Wars: Rise of the Resistance, 59
Steamboat Willie, 9, 53
Swiss Family Treehouse, 74, 78

Tiana's Bayou Adventure, 24–25
Tom Sawyer Island, 72–75
Toy Story, 28, 56–57
Tree of Life, 62–63, 64
Twilight Zone Tower of Terror, 54–56
Typhoon Lagoon, 82–83

Wilderness Explorers, 76, 94

ABOUT THE AUTHOR

HANNAH GRAMSON

Hannah Gramson has written books for kids of all ages. She visited Walt Disney World once many years ago. Her favorite rides were the Haunted Mansion and the Twilight Zone Tower of Terror.